Mentoring Matters

Mentoring Matters

A Toolkit for Organizing and Operating Student Advisory Programs

Mark D. Benigni and Sheryll Petrosky

ROWMAN & LITTLEFIELD EDUCATION

A division of

ROWMAN & LITTLEFIELD PUBLISHERS, INC.
Lanham • New York • Toronto • Plymouth, UK

Published by Rowman & Littlefield Education
A division of Rowman & Littlefield Publishers, Inc.
A wholly owned subsidiary of The Rowman & Littlefield Publishing Group, Inc.
4501 Forbes Boulevard, Suite 200, Lanham, Maryland 20706
http://www.rowmaneducation.com

Estover Road, Plymouth PL6 7PY, United Kingdom

British Library Cataloguing in Publication Information Available

Library of Congress Cataloging-in-Publication Data

Benigni, Mark D., 1971–
Mentoring matters : a toolkit for organizing and operating student advisory programs /
Mark D. Benigni and Sheryll Petrosky.
    p. cm.
    ISBN 978-1-60709-939-0 (cloth : alk. paper) — ISBN 978-1-60709-940-6 (pbk. : alk.
paper) — ISBN 978-1-60709-941-3 (electronic)
    1. Mentoring in education. I. Petrosky, Sheryll, 1955– II. Title.
    LB1731.4.B44 2011
    373.1102—dc22   2010038724

Printed in the United States of America

To the mentees who have taught us how to live well, laugh often, and share much.

Contents

Acknowledgments

As Woodrow Wilson once said, "I not only use all the brains I have, but all I can borrow." Now is the time for us to thank all those individuals who shared their brains, thoughts, wisdom, and leadership. Completing this book has challenged our intellect, expanded our patience, inspired us, and left us with many I owe you's!

We give special thanks to our advisory team, Maureen Moylan, Matt Zdeb, and Bruce Miller. Their demanding style, honesty, and direct approach kept us on track and motivated. Not only were they instrumental in helping us finish this book, but they have always supported us and believed in the value and purpose of this book.

We also want to thank other colleagues who shared their knowledge and expertise with us. Scott Brown, who led numerous mentoring and advisory program trainings, reviewed our manuscript and offered constructive feedback and mentoring tips. Kerrigan Mahoney created engaging lessons for use with our students that are included in our book.

We give special thanks to Lisa Hicks for her confidence in us, her technology expertise, and her unwavering support of all our school initiatives. Lisa, you are one of those unique people who know how to bring out the best in others. You have made us better educators, better leaders, and most importantly, better people.

To our Cromwell and Berlin school families, thanks for taking the journey with us; it has been fun and most rewarding. To all our mentors, mentees, and friends, may life always bring you happiness and success.

And last but by no means least, we thank our families. Your trust, love, and never-ending support will always be greatly appreciated. To our own children and all the children who continually put our lives in perspective, thank you for reminding us that the important things in life are the connections we make with people.

Preface

As schools are trying to personalize the learning environment, connect with their students, and assure that every student has an adult mentor in the building, the need for school-based mentoring programs could not be greater. When creating their school districts' mentoring programs, authors Mark Benigni and Sheryll Petrosky could not find age-appropriate, current, user-friendly mentoring lessons. With limited financial and human resources, schools are searching for practical, innovative, and trial-tested resources. *Mentoring Matters* provides that.

The authors share their experiences building, implementing, and refining their mentoring programs. Sheryll Petrosky has been the Mentor Program director for the Cromwell public schools since 2006. She generates weekly lessons that are electronically distributed to all mentors in advance of the upcoming sessions. Mark Benigni has created Berlin High School's first school-based mentoring program in 2007. He has shared the program highlights and his learning experiences with other educators and school districts.

Secondary educators who are interested in starting a school-based mentoring program or in reenergizing their current efforts will benefit from this book. It provides the action plan and all the resources necessary to launch a school-based mentoring program. All of the weekly sessions necessary to run the program successfully through a full school year are included. Forty-eight 30-minute sessions are at the reader's disposal, ready for immediate implementation. All the hurdles and obstacles have been eliminated.

Introduction

As students are faced with more responsibility, greater challenges, and increased demands, the importance of getting to know them and making connections with them could not be greater. *The Commonwealth Fund* notes that negative feelings students have about themselves, poor relationships with family members, poor grades, hanging out with the wrong crowd, and getting in trouble at school are the five most prevalent problems faced by young people today. These problems are negatively impacting school performance, graduation rates, and postsecondary educational success. Mentoring programs are reversing this trend and changing student perspectives about school.

As schools are being asked to individualize learning experiences for all students, mentoring programs are gaining momentum and interest from educators, students, families, and caring communities. Individual Student Support Plans are being implemented in secondary schools across the country. Higher student expectations, collapsing of academic levels, increased state credit requirements, more competitive college admission standards, a greater number of students in need of support, and the advent of twenty-first-century learning skills have left secondary schools, and the students they serve, looking for creative ways to provide support and encouragement. Communities and families are counting on schools to reinforce their efforts at providing a moral compass for children. Mentoring programs facilitate those efforts.

The National Mentoring Partnership list the following youth-related problems and issues: peer pressure, substance abuse, sexuality and teenage pregnancy, child abuse and family violence, depression and suicide, nutrition and health care, social adjustment and time management, and career exploration and part time work. All of these topics are addressed in the mentoring lessons included in this book. The nation's colleges and the business community are looking for schools to provide students with the essential basic skills and the ability to work collaboratively in a team environment. Mentoring programs encourage and support academic excellence and create a collaborative team-learning experience in which students are comfortable sharing openly with one another and with the adult mentor.

Strong evidence supports that if students perceive that they are connected to an adult in the school and the school offers a supportive environment, students will improve their academic output and behavioral performance. The purpose of a successful mentoring program is to provide the climate for this to occur. All children should know that they have at least one adult in the school community who knows them personally. Schools have diverse staffs that can support students who present different interests and individual needs.

Schools that have implemented mentoring programs have experienced the following positive outcomes: increased contributions to the community; improved academic performance; improved attendance; fewer tardies, suspensions, and referrals; less vandalism; improved respect and tolerance toward others; and improved school climate. Mentoring programs are helping communities form successful young adults who become contributive members of society. As communities are emphasizing the importance and value of volunteerism and civic involvement, mentoring programs are fostering the concept of giving back. Students and school staff will benefit from this mentoring journey.

WHY ESTABLISH A FORMAL MENTORING PROGRAM

Formal mentoring programs help build positive school climates and provide academic and emotional support for students. School-based mentoring is a comprehensive, regularly scheduled small-group meeting time that provides students with lessons and activities that connect them with their adult mentor, fellow mentees, and their school. These experiences are part of a formal curriculum that provides students with timely topical discussion items to ensure a supportive learning environment for all students.

Three years of school results from a comprehensive public high school show that students are "connecting" with their school-based mentors. In 2007, 61 percent of students reported they connected with their mentor. In 2008, with the same students participating with their mentor from the previous year, 82 percent of students reported that they connect with their adult mentor. In 2009, the results went up to 83 percent. These data confirm the need, and support the value, of school-based mentoring programs. Be committed to the mentoring journey and within three years your school will have a mentoring program that fosters student, staff, and peer connections. Don't be deterred by resistant staff members or unenthusiastic students. With the guidance and support of this mentoring manual any school can experience success.

Some of the most successful mentors had major reservations about implementing a mentoring or advisory program. Over time and through positive experiences with students, many of these staff members come to appreciate the value and importance of establishing mentoring programs. One well-respected veteran teacher stated, "Connections? I was going to do Connections? I am a teacher, not a connector! That is what I thought, [but] the reality was quite different. Within two months of working with them, a student in my group came to me. [He was] upset that he was going to have a fight and had no adult to turn to at home. The situation was diffused, and [now] every time the student passes by me in the hall, I always get a smile and a hey. I must say I was surprised at the level of trust that developed [between us] in such a short period of time." This teacher has become a mentor to students as well as to other staff members.

Another effective teacher and successful coach who questioned the need and value of school mentoring stated, "I've built very meaningful relationships with my Connections group. These are the type of relationships I could never build in the classroom or even on the practice field as a coach. The time allotted for Connections is an opportunity for students to unwind and forget about academics and focus on other issues that are relevant to the student at that particular time. We even take pictures and share stories during the summer via e-mail, so we are literally connected for the entire calendar year. I will truly miss the Connections group when they graduate." The good news is that another group of mentees will be ready to greet this teacher next year.

The value of mentoring has been openly expressed by appreciative students and supportive staff. One AP English teacher stated, "It is so refreshing to just spend time talking to students and getting to know them without the burden of assessment and grades attached to the relationship. It's amazing how quickly students were willing to open up and talk about things that are really important to their lives." This is where the real connections between mentors and mentees are fostered and nurtured. Building the relationship comes first, and improved academic performance and better behavior follow.

Other mentors expressed initial concern about mentee discomfort and lack of open communication. One teacher stated, "I really enjoy my Connections group. The kids I meet with were so nervous in the beginning of the year as freshmen. I have watched them begin to blossom as young adults. Having time in the day to meet with kids with no academic demands is refreshing. It helps keep me up to date with what is going on in the world of teenagers and it gives the kids someone safe to talk to about their problems." This mentor now feels more knowledgeable about technology, teen peer pressure, and the demands placed on a typical student, because of the authentic mentoring experience.

One mentor who expressed initial hesitation about the purpose of particular lesson plans stated, "I will be sad to see my Connections students graduate this year. In the past three years we have formed a family bond and look forward to seeing one another every week. No topic—school or personal—is taboo in our group; we feel free to express ourselves." Part of a school's mission is to empower students to feel comfortable and free to express themselves openly in and through different mediums. Mentoring provides that opportunity.

One mentor, who was viewed as an exceptional subject matter expert, was insulted that he was expected to mentor students. He stood up at a faculty meeting and claimed that this was a complete waste of his time. After three years with the same Connections group, this mentor has recently stated, "Connections has been an awesome experience for me and the kids I have had. We cannot wait to see each other. We have celebrated birthdays, getting into college, and other events. A lot of discussions about school and life in general have occurred. There has been a connection between the kids, and the kids and myself. The kids feel comfortable talking and they enjoy having a place to come to when they need assistance." Mentoring programs have made believers out of naysayers because the positive results speak for themselves. Student learning is enhanced by mentoring partnerships.

WHAT THIS BOOK PROVIDES

This resource book provides readers with the rationale and action plan for beginning a mentoring program at their school or for supplementing their current efforts. With this mentoring manual in hand, mentors and mentees will have 48 30-minute lessons ready to be implemented. The lessons are trial-tested and ready to be shared with students. This book provides the program, from actual lessons, to the framework, to the strategies for successful implementation.

The highlight of this mentoring manual is the weekly mentoring lessons that are organized for a full academic year. These activities provide engaging instructional topics that can be implemented in schools at any time. These lessons serve as the foundation of a successful mentoring program. From Facebook to bullying to teenage stressors, this book is comprehensive in its approach. If a topic is on a teenager's radar screen, a concern of the community, or a recurring school issue, a lesson plan to address the topic and provide support is included in this book.

SETTING THE FRAMEWORK

Change is never easy. People's natural instinct is to just say no to change. Yet change is essential in order to meet the academic and emotional needs of all students. Teachers need to first know why mentoring matters. That is where the discussion must begin. By valuing teacher time, current traditions, and associated fears, educators can successfully implement mentoring programs. Keeping it simple eliminates those fears.

So now what? Use this book to create a school-based mentoring program for all students in your school. By placing students in a small group with a caring adult mentor, schools can help meet the needs of students. By allocating time on a weekly basis within current schedules, mentoring will have a formal place in the school week. By recognizing time constraints in handling schoolwide initiatives and increased responsibilities, this resource book provides user-friendly mentoring sessions that are ready for immediate use. Just direct your mentees to pull out their mentoring manuals and turn to the desired lesson page. It truly is that easy!

When scheduling the time, mentor program coordinators should share the benefits of school-based mentoring with the staff, students, and families. An explanation of how this time can be effectively utilized by guidance and class advisors for special assemblies, all class meetings, and guidance activities must be understood by and shared with school staff. By utilizing mentoring time for these important activities, students will rarely miss out on authentic class learning experiences.

By asking staff for open and honest input at the onset of program implementation, schools will maximize their potential to get everyone on board. Mentor staff will remain with their mentees throughout their tenure at school. Staff should be provided with an opportunity to choose their preferred grade level. Public relations efforts should include notification, explanation, and documentation of success. This information should be disseminated to students, staff, parents, Board of Education members, and the community at large through school websites, mass e-mails, parent forums, student council meetings, faculty meetings, and Board of Education presentations.

When selecting mentoring groups, it is recommended that schools keep students with peers who are in their same grade level. All school staff members can be valuable, effective mentors. Certified staff, as well as noncertified staff, should be utilized to keep the mentoring groups as small as possible. A nurse, hall monitor, resource paraprofessional, or secretary can be an excellent student mentor. When dividing students into their grade-level groups, do not divide them alphabetically. Alphabetical grouping is probably used for many other school groupings already.

Know who is in charge. Is there a mentor coordinator or is the process administratively led? Our experiences show that mentoring programs are received better by staff when led by one of their colleagues. Providing an additional planning period and/or a small stipend is recommended for the mentoring coordinator. A mentoring coordinator is a current staff member who shares the rationale and purpose of mentoring with staff, students, and the community; creates and disseminates weekly lessons; and supervises and manages all mentoring groups. A mentor coordinator should be a current teacher who believes in the value and benefits of mentoring, has superior organizational skills, and has garnered the respect of the staff and students.

Mentors must know who the go-to person is. Someone has to be responsible and accountable for successful program implementation and active student participation. Mentoring coordinators fill this role. They are responsible for any change in mentor groups and for assigning administrators to take groups as well. By reviewing mentor groups before they are released to students and staff, potential student-to-student and student-to-staff difficulties can be avoided. Group changes should be made with great discretion and only when the mentor-mentee relationship is seen as irreparable.

PROCESS STEPS

Implementing lesson plans should be made mentor friendly. Having mentees utilize their personal mentoring handbook can maximize the mentoring time and facilitate further student reflection. Have students read the quotation of the day and discuss the meaning behind the words. Always leave time at the end of the session for wrap-up and roundtable discussion. Some lessons are designed for student reflection and assessment of performance. Reflection and assessment should be kept in student folders for periodic review of individual student progress. Program comprehension and an understanding of mentor roles are essential. Formal training is not required or necessary. Staff working in schools should know how to work with young people. That should be the basic expectation for any adult working with children. Building positive relationships and creating a collaborative school environment begins with the first mentoring session.

Mentoring topics should be sought from parents, staff, students, and the community at large. Some lessons are themed and should be delivered sequentially. Seasonal topics and current events may dictate topic scheduling. Lessons should be delivered weekly in order to facilitate positive, consistent connections between mentors and mentees. If a mentor is uncomfortable with a particular topic, another mentor could facilitate the lesson, the group could be combined with another mentoring group, or an alternative plan may be considered. If a topic guides a group discussion in another valuable direction, allow the students to chart the group mentoring course. Successful mentoring programs rely on the professional integrity of the mentors and the mutual respect of the mentees.

SUPPORTING ALL STUDENTS

These lessons can easily be differentiated to meet the needs of all students. Current staff members need to be utilized effectively to support a diverse student body that has different social, emotional, and academic needs. Students with attention issues may benefit from serving in mentoring group leadership roles. Students with intellectual disabilities may benefit from lesson modeling and guided practice. The book allows students and staff to preview future lessons to make sure that all group members feel comfortable and prepared for the formal mentoring session.

By creatively scheduling mentors and mentees, schools can target and support the students who have specific needs. Students with significant disciplinary concerns can be teamed with a school administrator. Students dealing with significant emotional issues might be partnered with the school social worker's mentoring group. The diverse talents and interests of school staff members should ensure that the individual needs of the students are properly addressed. Mentoring programs can help prepare students for successful inclusion in classes as well as in co-curricular school activities.

STRATEGIES FOR SUCCESS

Make mentoring feel different than a typical classroom experience. Arrange the room differently and have students leave their book bags and learning materials to the side. This is a time to decompress and connect with others. Mentors will enjoy the experience more if they participate in the activities with their mentees, and share their own ideas and answers with the group. Mentors should keep a personal folder for each mentee that contains academic progress lessons, report cards, and other pertinent information. These folders will be a compilation of mentee progress updates and will stay with the student's mentor until graduation. Graduating mentees will receive their folder so they can refer to the challenges overcome and the successes experienced. It is all about building positive rapport with students.

When beginning a mentoring session, mentors should do a quick check to see how mentees are feeling. All sessions will begin by sharing the quote of the day and asking mentees what the quote means to them. Discussion can flourish by simply asking each mentee to share something good that happened to him or her that day. By starting each session with something positive, mentors will increase their chances of having a successful mentoring session. When mentoring sessions are not successful, mentors may need to listen more than they speak.

General mentoring rules must be consistent among groups, and shared and respected by mentors and mentees. All mentees must attend sessions and attendance should be taken. All mentees must participate in the session activities and avoid outside reading, listening to music, or completing homework assignments. One person should speak at a time, side conversations must be avoided, and gossiping and rumor spreading must not be tolerated. If there is any mention of abuse or threats to immediate safety, mentors must report it to the appropriate authorities immediately.

Mentors can develop a positive rapport with their mentees by e-mailing them to welcome them back to school, celebrating birthdays, sharing favorite foods, and creating a mentoring group e-mail distribution list. Mentees can also volunteer to facilitate the lesson plan implementation and offer topic suggestions at the conclusion of any mentoring session. Some of the most successful and engaging lessons come from student recommendations.

There are numerous methods to equitably group all mentees, and to avoid repeating the same groupings again and again. The idea is to get mentees up and moving and actually talking to each other and having fun! Once mentors have mentees lined up, mentors can divide the groups by utilizing one of the following strategies:

- Count off by the number of groups needed.
- 1, 2, 1, 2.
- To establish pairs, tell mentees to line up in front of the class. Have them count off "1, 2, 3," up to half the number in the class, and then repeat. Match up the two number 1's, the two number 2's, etc.
- Tell mentees to stand up in a line based on birthdates. Then mentors can count off as they wish.
- Group them by the colors that they are wearing or their favorite colors.
- Group them by height.
- Group them by favorite sports, ice cream, music, etc.
- Line them up by number of siblings (most to least) and then decide how to split them up.
- Line them up by what they think is the ideal month for a wedding.
- Line them up by what they think is the ideal age to get married (youngest to oldest).

- Line them up by alphabetical order of middle names (A–Z).
- Line them up by the time they get up on Saturdays (earliest to latest).
- Line them up by number of cousins they have (least to most).

Don't wait. Now is the time to implement a school mentoring program. The sessions are planned, prepared, and tested. The staff is ready, and the students need the support. In order to successfully meet the needs of all students, provide students with twenty-first-century learning skills, and prepare students for postsecondary educational programs, schools must build relationships with their students and provide personalized educational programs. Mentoring programs help build relationships that improve student academic output as well as behavioral performance.

Schools with successful mentoring programs are reporting positive school climates and improved student performance. The documented benefits of school mentoring have made it imperative for schools to implement formal programs. The following lessons provide weekly activities that are easy for staff to implement and enjoyable for students. The quote of the day, student discussions, and well-designed activities are ready for you to implement today. All students will benefit from adult mentors who have engaging, educational, and enriching topics at their fingertips. Good luck and enjoy the journey!

I'd Like to Get to Know You

Use what you have to run toward your best—that's how I now live my life.

—Oprah Winfrey

Objective: To begin to get to know each other and increase everyone's comfort level to allow for productive discussions.

Materials needed: Copies of "People Search" worksheet, one for each mentee and one for yourself.

Procedure: Explain to mentees that this is a new program for all. (Mentors should introduce the program and explain what the purpose is.) The goal is *to make connections between and among students and adults in the school and the community*. The mentoring concept comes from the idea that connections can be made between students and adults, between students and students, and between students, adults, and the community as a whole over time.

Today's activity is called People Search. The directions are simple. No person can sign more than once. All are participating. (Distribute the questionnaires. Allow about twelve minutes). Come back to the group and discuss.

Discussion questions:
- Who saw a movie more than twice?
- What movie? How many times?
- Who has met someone famous?
- Who were they?
- What concerts have you attended?

Ask if anyone has any questions or concerns.

Closure questions:
• What is the purpose of a mentoring program?
• What was the reason for the people search?

1. Get one person to sign each square.
2. Try to use a person only once.

Table 1.1   People Search

Was born in another state: Which state:	Can wiggle his or her ears: Demonstrate:	Wears contacts: Clear or colored:
Has a job: Doing what:	Has been to another country: Which country:	Has met someone famous: Who and where:
Has been to a concert: Which did you attend last:	Knows how to say "I am hungry" in Spanish: How:	Can name three presidents whose last names begin with a "J": List:
Has been rock climbing: Where:	Has at least 3 siblings: How many and how old:	Has seen a movie more than twice: Which movie and how many times:

Hello, My Name Is. . . .

Every man I meet is in some way my superior.

—Ralph Waldo Emerson

Objective: To learn the names of the people in the group so that we can begin to have personal conversations.

Materials needed: None.

Procedure: This lesson should be done early in the year. Make sure people are sitting in new places around the circle. Start the activity by mentioning that this is an introduction activity. Tell each mentee to think of something that is unique to them, and that this should be something they are willing to share with the group. As the mentor, you will start by saying "Hi, I'm (mentor name) and I (something unique to mentor)." The next person in the circle will then say, "Hi, this is (mentor name) and he or she (unique thing)." The mentee will then state his or her name and what is unique about him or her. The next mentee in the circle will then reintroduce the mentor and the unique quality associated with him or her, the first mentee's name and his or her unique quality, and finally introduce himself or herself and the unique quality associated with him or her. This will go on until everyone has had the chance to share. Mentees might need prompting. Let the mentees figure it out. If time allows, ask if there is anyone who would volunteer (someone who only had one or two people to introduce at the beginning) to introduce the whole group by name and unique attribute.

Closure questions:
- Did you enjoy this activity? Why or why not?
- Why is this a necessary activity?
- Do your teachers know you by name? Is that a good or bad thing?
- At the end of the year, do you think you will know where everyone sat today?
- Why is that?
- What did it feel like to be the first to introduce yourself? The middle person? The last person?

Mastering Our Mission

Whatever course you decide upon, there is always someone to tell you that you are wrong. There are always difficulties arising which tempt you to believe that your critics are right. To map out a course of action and follow it to an end requires courage.

—Ralph Waldo Emerson

Objective: To assure all mentees are familiar with the school mission and to understand the purpose of their school community.

Materials needed: Copies of the school's mission and expectations.

Procedure: Go around the circle and ask mentees who Ray Kroc is. Let them guess before sharing his accomplishment with them. Continue until you have finished the list.

Discussion questions:
- What do all these people have in common? *Answer: A clear mission, high expectations, and a plan to get there.*
- Do you know the school's mission statement? *Distribute the mission statements.*
- Why is there a need for a mission and expectation statement? *Answers: To achieve success, understand the goal, etc.*
- Do you feel our school is meeting our mission? Why or why not?

Closure questions:
- What is a mission statement?
- Think of an advertising slogan. Share it with the group. Is this slogan an example of a mission statement? Why or why not?
- What can you as mentees do to help the school meet its mission?

Table 2.1

Person	Accomplishment
Ray Kroc	Started the McDonald's enterprise
LeBron James	Youngest basketball player for the Cleveland Cavaliers
Bill Gates	Started Microsoft
Donald Trump	Real estate developer and star of *The Apprentice*
Tiger Woods	Golfer
Shawn Corey Carter (Jay Z)	Rapper, songwriter, fashion designer
Oprah Winfrey	Talk show host, humanitarian, and media mogul

Where Am I Going?
How Will I Get There?

Action springs not from thought, but from a readiness for responsibility.

—Dietrich Bonhoeffer

Objective: To prepare for the future means demonstrating effort and commitment now.

Materials needed: One copy of the "Planning for Success" worksheet for each mentee, one folder for each mentee, and a piece of paper. *Mentee folders will be used throughout the year.*

Procedure: Distribute the "Planning for Success" worksheet and folder to each mentee. Have mentees complete the name, grade, projected graduation date, and schedule portions of the form. Inform them that after each major assessment (progress reports, report cards, etc.), they will be referring back to this form. Each form should be filled out neatly and as accurately as possible. Mentors will keep the forms and folders for the duration of the program. Encourage mentees to decorate their folders. Have mentees predict the grade they could reasonably achieve in each subject. Mentees should place their forms into their folders and return them to the mentor.

On a piece of paper, have mentees answer the following questions:

- What is your favorite subject? Why is it your favorite?
- What is your least favorite subject? Why is it your least favorite?
- Does any subject scare you? Why is that?

Closure: Explain to mentees that you will come back to this folder frequently over the year. This will allow them to see their progress over time. Preparing for the remainder of the year will help them focus.

Where Am I Going? How Will I Get There?

Planning for Success Worksheet

Name _____   High School _____
Birth date _____   Projected Graduation year _____
School Year _____
Circle one: Freshman – Sophomore – Junior – Senior
Complete the following for this school year.

List of enrolled classes	Targeted Grade	1st	2nd	3rd	4th	Year End
_____	_____	_____	_____	_____	_____	_____
_____	_____	_____	_____	_____	_____	_____
_____	_____	_____	_____	_____	_____	_____
_____	_____	_____	_____	_____	_____	_____
_____	_____	_____	_____	_____	_____	_____
_____	_____	_____	_____	_____	_____	_____
_____	_____	_____	_____	_____	_____	_____
_____	_____	_____	_____	_____	_____	_____

Learning Style(s): _____   Possible career choices: _____

_____

Extracurricular activities:

Let's Get Better Acquainted!

A pessimist sees the difficulty in every opportunity; an optimist sees the opportunity in every difficulty.

—Sir Winston Churchill

Objective: To get to know each other a little better and improve the social skills of mentees.

Materials needed: Note cards and pen/pencil.

Procedure: Distribute one note card to each mentee and tell them to write their name or nickname in the center of the note card.

On the top left part of the note card, have them answer this question:
   What was your favorite experience this past summer?

On the top right part of your note card, have them answer this question:
   Name one goal you have for yourself for this year.

On the bottom left, have them answer this question:
   If you could have dinner with anyone, dead or alive, who would it be?

On the bottom right, have them answer this question:
   When coming to school each day, what do you look forward to?

Have mentees pair up and share responses with each other.

Discussion questions:
• Why was that your favorite experience?
• Why did you choose that person to have dinner with?

Have mentees come back to the group and share one thing about their partner. If time allows, go around again and share another item.

Closure: Have one mentee summarize the purpose of this session. *Answer: To get to know each other.* See if the others in the group agree. If someone wishes to add or clarify something, allow them to.

Getting to Know Me

The highest reward for a person's toil is not what they get for it, but what they become by it.

—John Ruskin

Objective: To recognize personal strengths and to use that information to improve school performance.

Materials needed: Copy of the "What Kind of a Student Are You?" survey for each mentee, a pencil, and mentee folders.

Procedure: Distribute a survey to each mentee and have them fill it out. Encourage honesty as the information provided is for personal use. Have each mentee tally his or her results. When completed, place the survey and results in the mentee file.

Closure questions:
- Did your results surprise you?
- What in particular surprised you?
- What were your areas of strength?
- What is the one thing you could commit to in order to improve your performance?
- Do you see a connection between your survey scores and your academic grades?

What kind of a student are you????

To find out what kind of a student you are, read the following 10 questions and put check marks in the spaces that best describe you. This will only take a few minutes. **Be honest!**

		Always	Sometimes	Never
1.	I complete homework assignments.	_____	_____	_____
2.	I have all necessary materials when I go to class (book, pencil, etc.).	_____	_____	_____
3.	I use the time teachers give me in class to get started on homework.	_____	_____	_____
4.	I take good notes.	_____	_____	_____
5.	I ask and answer questions in class.	_____	_____	_____
6.	I use tricks to memorize information.	_____	_____	_____
7.	After reading an assignment in a textbook, I know what I've read.	_____	_____	_____
8.	I get along well with my teachers.	_____	_____	_____
9.	I am good at taking tests.	_____	_____	_____
10.	I am happy with my grades.	_____	_____	_____

Give yourself 2 points for each *ALWAYS* response, 1 point for each *SOMETIMES* response, and 0 for each *NEVER* response. Add up your score.

What your score means

20 – 15 points: You are a very good student. Future conversations about getting better grades will be a review for you. They could, however, help you raise your grades even higher.

14 – 10 points: You are a student who could be getting better grades. You will be able to improve your grades significantly.

9 – 5 points: You're probably not getting very good grades. The ideas we will be discussing can help you change that. It could even change how you feel about school.

4 – 0 points: Your grades must be a disaster. MEMORIZE everything we talk about!!!!

These are **tools** that can help improve your grades. Every day is a new beginning.

Do You Hear Me?

When people talk, listen completely. Most people never listen.

—Ernest Hemingway

Objective: To identify ways in which we communicate verbally and non-verbally and to recognize that we can deliver powerful messages without uttering a word.

Materials needed: None.

Procedure: Have mentees count off by twos (*one, two, one, two*). Line up—one line of ones, one line of twos. Mentees should be facing each other.

Activity 1. Have the ones think of a favorite vacation or concert. Each will be describing this experience with their hands behind their backs. The twos will be the listeners but will not comment verbally in any way. Time this activity for two minutes. When time is up, process what happened.

Discussion questions:
- How did you feel during this experience?
- What was it like to speak with your hands behind your back?
- How did it feel to speak to someone who gave you no verbal response?
- Listeners, how did you feel?
- How did you, as listeners, let the person know you were listening?

Activity 2. While still in these lines, have the twos think of a favorite gift they received. Tell the twos that they will be describing the gift and why it was their favorite to the ones. Tell the ones that they are to completely ignore the speakers. Time this for two minutes. When you have finished timing, process what happened.

Discussion questions:
- How did you feel during this experience?
- What was it like, number twos, to be completely ignored?
- How did you, the non-listeners, feel about ignoring the speakers?

Activity 3. Mentees are still in line. Number ones, think of a television show that you like. Describe the show to the number twos. Number twos should listen, but not have *any* eye contact with the person. Time this for two minutes. When time is up, process what happened.

Discussion questions:
- How was it to talk with someone who made no eye contact?
- Listeners, did you try to sneak a peek at the person speaking?

Activity 4. Have the number twos think of their favorite musician/singer/group. Then have them choose one of their favorite songs. Have them explain why that is their favorite song. Number ones should look at their partner, but their body language should clearly say, "I'm not listening." Time this for two minutes. When time is up, process what happened.

Discussion questions:
- How did you feel during this?
- Did you feel listened to? Why or why not?

Closure:

Have mentees share examples of non-verbal methods of communication. Mentees may role-play these examples.

Are You Still Listening?

Children today are tyrants. They contradict their parent, gobble their food, and tyrannize their teachers.

—Socrates

Objective: To practice active listening skills and to improve communication.

Materials needed: Note cards or small pieces of paper, and pencils or pens.

Procedure: Ask mentees to identify different methods of communication. *Answers: Eye contact, body language, verbal responses, etc.* Read the quote of the day. Ask mentees who the author was. Did that come as a surprise? Would their parents/guardians agree with Socrates?

Then ask mentees to write the answers to the following questions on the paper.

- Name one person you admire or look up to.
- Name one thing you *want* people to think about you.
- Name one thing, realistic or not, you would like to be when you grow up.
- Name one thing you are proud of.

Have mentees count off by 3's or 4's depending on the size of the group. Each group should have three people. Have each mentee share their answers within the smaller group. After 4 or 5 minutes, stop the activity. Have mentees put their cards out of sight. One person in each group should turn their chair around so that they are facing away from the others. The two remaining mentees in each group will now share what they learned about the person facing outward. After each mentee within the group has had a turn, bring all the groups back to the circle.

25

Discussion questions:

- Did the speakers share correct information about the mentee facing away from the group?
- How did it feel to have people talking about you while you were facing outward?
- Even though they were sharing your responses, were you comfortable with it?
- Which question was the hardest to answer? Why?
- What did you learn from this experience?
- How would you feel if what was said about you was *not* the response you gave?
- Has this type of thing ever happened to you—hearing someone say you said something when you did not?

Closure:

Listening requires practice to be sure that what is said is what is heard. How can you make certain that what you hear is what is being said? *Answers: By clarifying responses, watching body language, concentrating on what is being said, and so on.*

Talk This Way

Do what you can, with what you have, where you are.

—Theodore Roosevelt

Objective: To understand that communicating includes clarifying.

Materials needed: One copy of the figure shown on the next page and paper and pencils for mentees.

Procedure: Ask for a volunteer who believes he or she possesses strong communication skills. That person will have his or her back to the group. He or she will be given a diagram that he or she is going to attempt to get the group to draw based on verbal instructions only! The group cannot ask for clarification. The describer cannot ask the group for any feedback. The only person talking is the describer.

Give the person the copy of the figure shown at the bottom of the page. Be sure not to let anyone else see it.

Have him or her turn his or her back to the group.

When he or she is finished, have him or her turn around and see what his or her group has drawn.

Discussion questions:
- What frustrated you about this activity?
- Did the describer use language you understood?
- Did the describer give you enough information or too little information?
- What do you think of when you hear the word *chopper? Some might think helicopter, others might think motorcycle.*
- Why is language so important in communication?

Closure questions:
• What did you learn about listening in this session?
• Why is clarification important?

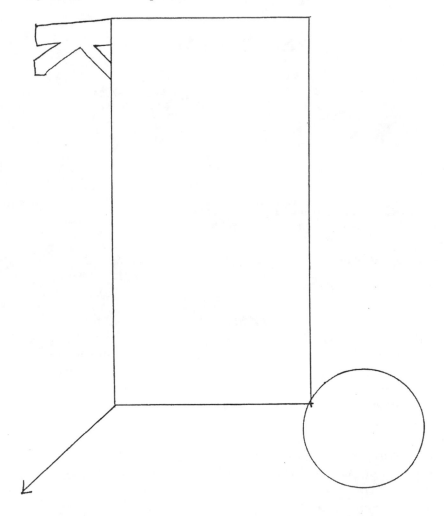

Shhh . . . No Noise, Please!

Kind hearts are the gardens;
Kind thoughts are the roots;
Kind words are the flowers;
Kind deeds are the fruits.

—English Proverb

Objective: To recognize the importance of silence.

Materials needed: Note cards and pens.

Procedure: Ask each mentee to write down what they would be if they were

- a piece of fruit.
- a historical figure.
- a household object.
- a cartoon character.
- any other off-the-wall category you can think of.

Return to the circle. Go around the circle and ask each mentee what choice he or she made for a piece of fruit. Continue through the list of choices. This is a warm-up activity, and the next activity will require restraint.

This activity is called "Solemn and Silent." Explain that this exercise takes self-control. Pair mentees back to back. On the count of three, everyone must face their partner, look each other in the eyes, and then try to remain solemn and serious. No speaking! The first to smile or laugh must sit down. All who remain standing then take a new partner and the activity continues until only one person has not smiled or laughed. (Second round of playing can involve two teams competing to outlast each other.) If in the end there is a pair who are keeping straight faces, the rest of the group can act as hecklers to disrupt them.

Closure questions:
• How did you react when someone smiled or laughed? Were you the initiator of the smile or laugh?
• Are you comfortable in quiet environments? Why or why not?
• If you are in the car and no one is talking, how do you respond?
• If you ask a question and the answer is silence, what do you think?
• Does silence feel the same for all people?
• How can silence be used effectively when communicating?

Make the *Right* Choice

Ethics, too, are nothing but reverence for life. This is what gives me the fundamental principle of morality, namely, that good consists in maintaining, promoting, and enhancing life, and that destroying, injuring, and limiting life are evil.

—Albert Schweitzer

Objective: To encourage mentees to make ethical decisions even when no one is watching. This will help them make ethical decisions in other situations.

Materials needed: Paper and pencil.

Procedure: Have mentees write their answers to these questions on a sheet of paper.

What would you do if

- you saw someone hit a car and take off?
- you hit a car and no one saw you do it?
- you realized you were undercharged when you made a purchase?
- you saw another student copy someone's homework?
- you saw a peer cheat on a test that you had studied very hard for?
- you saw someone stealing from the cafeteria?
- you saw a student crying in the hall?

Go bullet by bullet and ask for responses. Mentees do not *have* to respond. After completing the task clarify the expression "ethical decisions."

Ethical decisions are decisions you make pertaining to or dealing with morals. They are decisions made in accordance with rules or standards for right conduct or practice.

Discussion questions:
- What are some standards that we all agree on?
- What would our school look like if everyone made ethical decisions?
- What kinds of ethical decisions have you had to make?
- How does it feel when you make a decision that you know is wrong?
- How does it feel when you make a decision that you know is right?
- Give examples from sports or entertainment of unethical decisions.
- Did those examples of unethical decision change how you looked at that person?

Closure activity:
Go around the circle and have mentees make one comment in answer to the question: What challenges face a person who makes an ethical decision? Go around the circle again and ask for one positive thing that a person experiences when he or she makes an ethical decision. *Examples: feeling good, satisfied, relieved, and so on.*

Let's See If What I *Thought* I Was Doing Matches Up with What I *Did*

Success is simple. Do what's right, the right way, at the right time.

—Arnold H. Glasgow

Objective: To reflect and assess so that improvement can take place.

Materials needed: Report cards or progress reports (from guidance), schedules (in mentee folders), and copies of the "Self-Assessment" forms, one for each mentee.

Procedure: Redistribute the mentee folders. Distribute the "Self-Assessment" forms. You will be meeting with each mentee individually. Have the mentee bring the form with him or her. If a self-improvement plan is being designed, have the mentee write the plan down. These meetings should be brief to allow mentees to reflect on, assess, and strategize for improvement. If a mentee is already successful, have a discussion on extracurricular activities. Please follow the following guidelines:

- Have students bring their self-evaluation up with them.
- Be *sensitive* to the situation.
- Keep the discussion *private*. Have mentees in one section of the room and the individual meetings in another.
- The conversation should be 1–2 minutes long per mentee.

Discussion questions:
- What surprised you the most? Why?
- What was your most challenging class? Why?
- What was your favorite class? Why?

• What is one goal you have for improving next term?
• What activities are you involved in?

Closure:

Staple each mentee's self-reflection and report card together and place them in the mentee folder for future reference.

Self-Assessment Worksheet

HOW AM I DOING?

Name _____   Date _____

Projected Graduation Year _____

Objective: To assess your progress after each major evaluation.

For your planning, answer the following questions:

What courses am I doing well in?	Why? What went *right*?

What courses am I having difficulty with?	Why? What went wrong? How can I improve?

Self-Assessment Worksheet

Here are two things I will do to improve or maintain my work.

1.

2.

Any other comments, suggestions, or concerns?

Get S-M-A-R-T

By recording your goals and dreams on paper, you set in motion the process of becoming the person you most want to be.

—Mark Victor Hansen

Objective: To inform mentees of the importance of goal setting and to create a personal S-M-A-R-T goal.

Materials needed: One copy of the "Goal-Setting" worksheet for each mentee, pencil, and mentee folder.

Procedure: Explain to mentees that goal setting will be the topic for this session. In order for something to be a goal

- it has to be important to you, personally.
- it has to be within your power to make it happen through your own actions.
- it has to be something you have a reasonable chance of achieving.
- it must be clearly defined and have a specific plan of action.

Read the quote of the day.

Discussion questions:
- Who is the author? *He wrote the series of books "Chicken Soup for the Soul."*
- What is the significance of the quote?

Explain to mentees that they will now begin the task of setting goals. This is one method for goal setting. It is not the only one. (You can share a goal you have set for yourself. Explain how you went about achieving that goal, or how you modified it and why.)

Ask mentees to consider an academic or civic goal for themselves. They do *not* have to share their ideas, but choosing a goal that is reasonable and measurable is important.

One method of goal setting is the S-M-A-R-T method.

S—*Specific.* A specific goal has a greater chance for success: not "I'm going to get in shape," but "I'm going to go to a gym and work out three times a week."

Answer the six "W" questions.

- *Who* is involved?
- *What* do I want to accomplish?
- *Where* will I accomplish this?
- *What* is a reasonable time frame?
- *Which* identifies requirements and constraints on the goal.
- *Why* gives specific reasons, benefits, or purpose for the goal.

M—*Measurable.* See if progress is being made so that you can track your goal.

A—*Attainable.* Goals are attainable as you move closer toward them. As you expand and grow, your goals seem closer.

R—*Realistic.* To be realistic, your goal must be something you are *willing* and *able* to work toward. You also must *believe* you can do it.

T—*Tangible.* A tangible goal can be experienced through your senses—that is, taste, touch, smell, sight, or hear. If you can see you are making progress, you will hear good things. Then, intangible goals become tangible goals. An example of a tangible goal is "I will improve by one letter grade in algebra by the end of the school year."

Closure activity:

Have mentees create one personal academic S-M-A-R-T goal using the worksheet. When mentees have finished, place each goal in the mentee folders.

Goal-Setting Worksheet

Name _____   Date _____

A S-M-A-R-T goal must be

S—*specific* answers to the questions *who, what, when, where, why, and how.*

M—*measurable,* meaning you can see your progress.

A—*attainable,* which means you can see your movement toward your goal.

R—*realistic,* meaning you can do it.

T—*tangible,* that is, you can see your way there.

Write a personal academic or social goal in the space provided. You might use your "Self-Assessment" worksheet to help you decide what your goal should be.

_____

_____

_____

Now answer these questions:

Is your goal *specific?*

Is your goal *measureable?*

Is your goal *attainable?*

Is your goal *realistic?*

Is your goal *tangible?*

If the answer to all of these questions is yes, your goal is a S-M-A-R-T one. If you answered no to any of these questions, rewrite your goal.

Place this form in your file.

What Is Important to Me?

Values provide perspective in the best of times and the worst.

—Charles Garfield

Objective: To identify what is valued.

Materials needed: A copy of the "Values-Setting" worksheet, a pencil, and a sheet of plain paper that can be cut into pieces for each mentee.

Procedure: Distribute the materials to each mentee. Have the mentees divide their blank sheet of paper into twelve strips (they do not need to be neat as they will be writing on them.) You may also do this ahead of time for expediency. Begin by explaining that you will say a word and mentees should write it on one of their twelve pieces of paper. They should then take that paper and place it on the matrix in the position they value it (#1 is the most important and #12 is the least important). Continue to do this until all twelve pieces of paper are used and all twelve spaces are filled. (Mentors, be sure to allow some time in between as mentees will be repositioning their papers. Try it yourself!)

- Money
- A nice home
- Friends
- Education
- Spiritual beliefs
- A job you love
- A good-paying job
- Love
- Family

- Health
- Happiness

The last piece of paper is a bonus. Mentees can write anything they want to on that piece.

Ask mentees to look over their list and see if they are satisfied.

Discussion questions:
- What did you place in the #1 position?
- How many times did you have to rearrange your matrix?
- Why did you need to rearrange?
- Do you think that this order will change during your life?
- Do you think it can change from week to week?
- Why is that?

Closure questions:
- Do you see your order remaining the same after you graduate from high school?
- Why do you think that is?
- Will you still value the same things but maybe not in the same order?

Table 15.1   Values-Setting Worksheet

#1 *(Most important)*	#7
#2	#8
#3	#9
#4	#10
#5	#11
#6	#12 *(Least important)*

Pay It Forward—Part 1

When we feel love and kindness toward others, it not only makes others feel loved and cared for, but it helps us also to develop inner happiness and peace.

—The Dalai Lama

Objective: To demonstrate how acts of kindness can make a world of difference in someone's life and explore ways of demonstrating kindness in our lives.

Materials needed: Access to a computer and the Internet.

Procedure: Be sure the YouTube links are still available.

Watch this touchy-feely video:

www.youtube.com/watch?v=uvG1iVw8IjQ

Or a clip from the movie *Pay It Forward*:

www.youtube.com/watch?v=tGcwG-2owow

Discussion questions:
- What stood out to you the most about this video?
- Are there any images that you remember? Why?
- What words were repeated the most? What idea does this emphasize?
- What was the overarching message in the video?
- Why is it an important message?
- How does it relate to your life?

Have the mentees go around the room and share something nice that someone has done for them.

With a partner, ask mentees to brainstorm a list of nice, out-of-the-ordinary actions they could do for someone else. Each group should share their best ideas.

Ask mentees if they would be willing to try to do something that they would not ordinarily do for someone else to help them have a better day. The group should decide what guidelines they are comfortable with as a group, if any. (Encourage them to think beyond their own friends and family—for example, seniors could do something for a freshman they have never met before.)

Closure:

Tell mentees that they will be reporting their personal progress next week, as this topic will be continued.

—*Submitted by Kerrigan Mahoney*

Pay It Forward—Part 2

It is every man's obligation to put back into the world at least the equivalent of what he takes out of it.

—Albert Einstein

Think of giving not as a duty but as a privilege.

—John D. Rockefeller Jr.

Objective: To encourage kindness and show that one person can make a difference in the lives of many just as one little penny can promote peace.

Materials needed: A projector and access to the Internet. Check to see that the Internet link is still available.

Procedure:
- Remind mentees of last week's session.
- Ask mentees to share their experiences doing something kind for someone else (they don't have to name names). If any mentees did not do anything particularly out of the ordinary, have them discuss why and then encourage them to try again (without pressure to discuss).
- Brainstorm with the mentees reasons why it is important to be kind that might go beyond the interactions between just two people. *Consider the school culture, the community at large, the state, the United States, and beyond.*
- Watch the following video about Greg Mortensen: abcnews.go.com/Video/playerIndex?id=7193877

Discussion questions:
- What stood out the most?
- What was the most surprising?

- How does this relate to the idea of doing something kind on a local or individual level?
- What is more important, the scale of an act or the act itself?

Have mentees write a short reflection on this two-week activity. Collect the reflections and place them in the mentees' folders.

Closure questions:
- Can acts of kindness make a difference?
- How does that change the "feel" of the environment?

—Submitted by Kerrigan Mahoney

Celebrating Our Similarities

We have become not a melting pot but a beautiful mosaic. Different people, different beliefs, different yearnings, different hopes, different dreams.

—Jimmy Carter

Objective: To see the similarities in each other to minimize prejudiced behavior.

Materials needed: A piece of construction paper for each mentee.

Procedure: Give all mentees one sheet of paper and ask them to close their eyes. Tell them to do the following:

- Fold paper in half.
- Fold in half again.
- Rip bottom left corner.
- Rip bottom right corner.
- Open up and hold the paper over your head.
- Open your eyes.

Discussion questions:

- What do you notice about your sheet of paper?
- What was the first thing you did when you opened your eyes? *Answer: Looked at your paper.*
- Did you look at other people's paper?
- Are they all the same? Why not?
- Is there a right or wrong way? *Answer: No, just different.*
- List the ways our school is different from ones you have previously attended.
- Are differences bad? Good?

- Cite some ways in which differences are good.
- Cite some ways in which differences are bad.

Closure questions:
- Go around the circle and ask mentees to name one way in which we (individuals in this group) are similar.
- How would this activity relate to diversity?
- How do people demonstrate prejudice—whether racist, ethnic, religious, etc?

A Leader, Please

Individual commitment to a group effort—that is what makes a team work, a company work, a society work, a civilization work.

—Vince Lombardi

Objective: To identify ways we communicate without using words and to identify emerging leaders when given a task.

Materials needed: None.

Procedure: Divide mentees into two groups of equal size. Without talking (appropriate hand gestures are acceptable) and as quickly as possible, have mentees arrange themselves according to the number of siblings each has (zero in front).

While still standing, debrief the activity.

Discussion questions:
• How did you communicate?
• Were the directions simple enough or too simple?

Without talking, have mentees arrange themselves in a straight line according to their birth month and date. Do not interfere with their process; let them silently work out this arrangement themselves. After mentees have finished, start at one end of the line and have each mentee say his or her birth month and date aloud to see if the group did what was expected. If the group was successful, ask these questions. If not, ask what happened.

Discussion questions:
• How did you communicate?
• Was this more complicated than the previous? Why?

A Leader, Please

The human pretzel

Set up and instructions

- Be aware that the activity may involve close physical proximity and touch in potentially sensitive places!
- Ask participants to form a circle, shoulder-to-shoulder. Encouraging/urging participants to stand closer can be a subtle way of helping them to prepare for what is about to come.
- Ask each participant to place one hand in the middle of the circle and to grab somebody else's hand. They should not grab the hand of someone to their immediate left or right.
- Ask participants to say hello to the person they are holding hands with.
- Then ask participants to put their other hand in the middle, grab a different person's hand, and say hello to that person.
- Don't let participants let go of hands. Some will be tempted to think the activity might be over, but it is only just starting.
- Instruct participants to untangle themselves, without letting go of hands, into a circle.
- There will be a mixture of reactions, often including nervous laughter, fun amusement, excitement, trepidation, strong suspicion that it cannot be done, and others who may view the task as a somewhat sadistic or inappropriate joke. Often some group members will have done the task before, but this does not really matter. The task is unique each time.
- Participants may change their grip so as to be more comfortable, but they should not to unclasp and reclasp so as to undo the knot.
- Explain that whenever the group members are talking to someone or about someone, that the person's first name must be used. This usually requires supervision and reinforcement by the instructor, but once enforced, it is excellent for learning names. It also usually helps the group to work together and find solutions, because their communications are more accurate with names involved.
- Stand back and see what happens.
- Be prepared to see little progress for quite some time. However, once the initial unfolding happens, the pace toward the final solution usually seems to quicken.
- If the task is completed quickly, have the group try again. Occasionally, the task seems too hard and participants seem to make almost no progress. Let them struggle for about 10 minutes, then offer the group one unclasp and reclasp. You can first have them discuss and decide what unclasp and reclasp would be most useful.

- Most of the time a full circle falls out, but occasionally there are two or even three interlocking circles. The task is complete when the knot is sorted into its simplest structure.

Closure questions:
- Did you feel uncomfortable in this activity? Why or why not?
- How did the pretzel activity relate to the initial activity? *Answers: Communication, working together, organizing to complete a task, etc.*
- How did your group communicate?
- Was it easier to perform a task when you could talk?
- Who was the leader in the pretzel task?
- How did you identify the leader?

What Does This Document Say about *Me?*

Don't lower your expectations to meet your performance. Raise your level of performance to meet your expectations. Expect the best of yourself, and then do what is necessary to make it a reality.

—Ralph Marston

Objective: To look at transcripts and see what a person "looks like" based on that document.

Materials needed: Copies of three transcripts from your school. White out all personal information. One transcript should be from a consistently strong junior or senior student, one from a junior who has shown improvement over time, and one from a struggling sophomore or freshman.

Procedure: Begin the discussion about transcripts with mentees by asking:
- How many of you have seen a high school transcript?
- If there are upper classmen, ask the following: How many of you have seen your high school transcript?

Explain to mentees that a high school transcript is a record of all the courses a person took in high school as well as his or her grades in those courses. It will also include the student's overall grade point average (GPA). High school transcripts are typically requested by colleges to make admission decisions. Sometimes other organizations and employers may request a copy of an individual's transcript to make certain types of decisions, but this occurs relatively infrequently. This official document is a picture of the student's time at this institution.

Display the first transcript (*strong academic student*).

Discussion questions:
- What do you think this student is like?
- What qualities would you say he or she possesses?
- If you were an employer, would you hire this person? Why?

Display the second transcript (*student who is improving over time*). Ask the same questions and then add:
- What does this transcript say about this student over time?

Display the third transcript (*student who is not that strong*). Ask the same questions and then add:
- What options do you think this student will have for college?
- What might his or her employee think of him or her?

Closure: Suggest to mentees that each should be aware of what their "high school picture" says about them. Ask mentees how they can redirect their energy to change this picture or add to it. *Answers: By looking at their self-assessment plans, writing a SMART goal, reflecting on the situation, etc.* Remind them that it is never too late!

Here Today, Gone Tomorrow!

You can't learn in school what the world is going to do next year.

—Henry Ford

Objective: To help identify things that are obsolete; this can help us predict the future and create realistic plans.

Materials needed: Board, markers, and Internet access if possible for display of obsolete objects.

Procedure: Ask the mentees what the following things are (from the item list in the table). If you have access to the Internet, you could have pictures of these objects on the computer to share with mentees and ask them what they are.

These items are obsolete. What does *obsolete* mean? (Allow mentees time to discuss the concept of something being obsolete).

The word *obsolete* means "no longer used." Ask for a volunteer to write what is said on the board. Have mentees brainstorm a list of things that might be obsolete in 10 years.

Here's an example to get you started: Write "movie theaters" on the board. Allow the mentees time to generate their list. Feel free to interject your ideas as well. This activity should take 5 to 10 minutes. Bring the group back to the circle.

Discussion questions:
- Why do you think these things will be obsolete?
- Why might they not be obsolete?
- What are some things in your house that you no longer use?
- Are they obsolete or not used? Does *obsolete* mean the same thing as *not used*?

Table 21.1

Item	Description
Rotary Phone	Circular dial with numbers that you have to dial. Phone numbers began with two letters.
Rabbit Ears	Antennae located on top of an old television to help get good reception.
Shorthand	A form of writing involving symbols that secretaries used instead of writing out the entire word.
Slide Rule	A long ruler-like item used to calculate complicated math problems (before calculators).
Percolator	A coffeemaker that sat on the stove and made, or "perked," coffee. It took 15 minutes to make a cup of coffee.
Transistor	A small battery-operated radio that received very few AM stations.
Girdles	The SPANDEX of years ago.
VCR	A precursor to a DVD player.

Closure questions:
- What item that you use today might be obsolete in 10 years?
- How will this knowledge help prepare you for the future?

Rules Are Rules . . . Or Are They?

If we don't discipline ourselves, the world will do it for us.

—William Feather

Objective: To recognize the need for some rules in our society and to understand why some school rules are necessary.

Materials needed: None.

Procedure: Have a mentee read the following scenarios and then proceed with the discussion questions.

Scenario #1:

Last year the fire department notified 75 candidates that they were chosen to be in the next class at the fire academy. Thousands of people had applied for these positions. On the first day they were to report, two candidates were late. When they arrived, they were told to leave and their positions were going to be given to two other people. The commander who spoke to them said, "When we need you, we mean *here,* not somewhere else. We mean *right now,* not later."

Discussion questions:
- Was the commander justified in dismissing them? Why or why not?
- The commander dismissed the two candidates in front of the entire class. Why did he do it this way?

Scenario #2:

A high school teacher tells her classes at the beginning of the year that if anyone has five or more unexcused absences during a marking period, they will fail that marking period. She adds that it does not matter if the student is doing well or not. Five or more unexcused absences during a marking period will mean failure. A student in first-period class misses five classes and the teacher sends a failure notice home. The student and her parents are shocked because she is an above-average student.

Discussion questions:
- Did the teacher clearly explain her policy?
- Did she have the right to do this?
- Was it a fair policy? Why or why not?
- Should rules ever be broken or redesigned? When or why?

Closure questions:
- Why do schools have an attendance policy?
- Why do schools have dress codes?
- What would you change about your school's policies if you could? Why?
- Are all rules school based? *Answer: No, there are also district rules, state rules, and federal rules.*
- What would happen if there were no rules?

Can We Both Be Right?

If you keep doing what you've always done, you'll always get what you've always gotten.

—John C. Maxwell

Objective: To identify respectful behavior so that we better demonstrate respect.

Materials needed: A piece of paper for each mentee, mentee folders, pencil or pen, a copy of the poem "RESPECT" by Don Wilson, found at www. poemhunter.com/poem/respect-36/

Procedure: Distribute a piece of paper to each mentee, to be used later in the activity. Explain to mentees that if they agree with a statement they should put their thumbs up for yes. If they disagree, thumbs down for no. Say:

- Do you think you could learn to fly a plane? (*thumbs up or down*)
- To ride a motorcycle? (*thumbs up or down*)
- Do you think you could learn to captain a boat or hang glide? (*thumbs up or down*)

Go from mentee to mentee and ask why each responded as he or she did. Responses should vary, but the key is, *these are skills that can be taught!*

- Is it possible to teach people to be respectful in spite of their differences?
- What are two ways in which you, personally, could be more respectful at school, during activities, or at home? (Pause and let them think. Have each mentee share an idea.)

Discussion questions:

- Do you think it is difficult to show respect when someone thinks differently from you? Why or why not?
- Do you think it might be difficult for someone to show you respect because you think differently than they do? Why or why not?
- What would it be like if everyone thought the same way, acted the same way, dressed the same way, liked the same food, enjoyed the same activities, etc?
- How would the school climate (*this term might require some discussion*) look if everyone in school (teachers, students, administrators, secretaries, cafeteria workers, bus drivers, hall monitors, etc.) demonstrated more respect toward each other?
- Would you enjoy school more? Would you, in turn, be more or less likely to get involved in things?
- Do you think school would be more productive?
- Think of an example, right here in our group, that might be an example of disrespect. (*Mentees do not have to actually share this, though they can.*) What was the reaction of the group? Now think of an example where respect was demonstrated. What was the reaction of the group?
- Just for today, make a commitment to be more respectful in one way. Write that one way down on the paper in front of you. Next time we meet, we will see how you did.

Closing activity: Write the word RESPECT on the board. Have each mentee write a "feeling" word around that word. Then have a mentee read the poem "RESPECT" by Don Wilson. Discuss its meaning.

Let's See If What I *Thought* I Was Doing Matches Up with What I *Did*

Success is simple. Do what's right, the right way, at the right time.

—Arnold H. Glasgow

Objective: To reflect and assess so that improvement can take place.

Materials needed: Report cards or progress reports (from guidance), schedules (in mentee folders), and copies of the "Self-Assessment" forms, one for each mentee.

Procedure: Redistribute the mentee folders. Distribute the "Self-Assessment" forms. You will be meeting with each mentee individually. Have the mentee bring the form with him or her. If a self-improvement plan is being designed, have the mentee write the plan down. These meetings should be brief to allow mentees to reflect on, assess, and strategize for improvement. If a mentee is already successful, have a discussion on extracurricular activities. Please follow the following guidelines:

- Have students bring their self-evaluation up with them.
- Be *sensitive* to the situation.
- Keep the discussion *private*. Have mentees in one section of the room and the individual meetings in another.
- The conversation should be 1–2 minutes long per mentee.

Discussion questions:
- What surprised you the most? Why?
- What was your most challenging class? Why?
- What was your favorite class? Why?

- What is one goal you have for improving next term?
- What activities are you involved in?

Closure:
Staple each mentee's self-reflection and report card together and place them in the mentee folder for future reference.

Self-Assessment Worksheet

HOW AM I DOING?

Name _____   Date _____

Projected Graduation Year _____

Objective: To assess your progress after each major evaluation.
For your planning, answer the following questions:

What courses am I doing well in?	Why? What went *right*?

What courses am I having difficulty with?	Why? What went wrong? How can I improve?

Here are two things I will do to improve or maintain my work.

1.

2.

Any other comments, suggestions, or concerns?

I See It . . . I Hear It . . . I Feel It . . .

Continuous effort—not strength or intelligence—is the key to unlocking our potential.

—Winston Churchill

Objective: To know your learning style means you can optimize your learning.

Materials needed: Copies of the learning style/intelligence checklist, mentee folders, and pencils

Procedure: Distribute copies of the learning style/intelligence checklist to mentees. Have them check those that apply to them. When they have finished, have mentees circle the area that received the most checks. Explain that that is their learning style.

- Verbal learners are "word smart." These learners pay close attention to what is said and often enjoy words, vocabulary, reading, grammar, and poetry. What kind of professionals can verbal learners become? *Answers: Lawyers, politicians, journalists, etc.*
- Logical/mathematical learners are "number smart." Number people like breaking things into pieces and reassembling them. They like order and sequence. Scientists, doctors, and physicists, for example, are logical learners.
- Spatial learners are "picture smart." These learners are very observant. They think in three dimensions; use metaphors; and prefer charts, graphs, pictures, and color. Artists, designers, and architects are generally spatial learners.

INTELLIGENCE CHECKLIST

VERBAL

___ Books are very important to me
___ I show an aptitude for word games like Scrabble or crossword puzzles
___ I entertain myself and others with tongue twisters, silly rhymes, or puns
___ Studying English, social studies and History comes easy to me
___ I can hear words in my head before I read, speak or write them down

LOGICAL/MATHEMATICAL

___ I can easily compute numbers in my head
___ Math and/or Science were among my favorite subjects in school
___ I enjoy playing games or solving brain teasers that require logical thinking
___ I sometimes think in clear, abstract, wordless imageless concepts
___ I am interested in new developments in science

SPATIAL

___ I often see clear visual images when I close my eyes
___ I prefer reading materials that are heavily illustrated
___ I frequently use a camera to record what is around me
___ I like to draw or doodle
___ Geometry was easier than algebra for me at school

KINESTHETIC

___ I find it difficult to sit for long periods of time
___ I engage in at least one sport or physical activity on a regular basis
___ I need to touch things in order to learn more about them
___ I would describe myself as well coordinated
___ I often enjoy to spend my free time outdoors

MUSICAL INTELLIGENCE

___ I can tell when a musical note is off key
___ I frequently listen to music on radio, CD's or other
___ I play a musical instrument
___ I often tap or hum melodies during everyday activities
___ I can keep time to a piece of music with a simple percussive instrument

INTERPERSONAL

___ I am the sort of person that people come to for advice
___ I prefer group or team sports
___ I have at least three very close friends
___ I feel comfortable in large crowds
___ I like to get involved in social gatherings at work, church or in the community

INTRAPERSONAL

___ I regularly spend time alone meditating, reflecting or thinking about important life questions
___ I have important goals about my life that I think about on a regular basis
___ I would prefer to spend a weekend alone in a cabin in the woods rather than at a fancy resort with lots of people around
___ I am self employed or have at least thought seriously about starting my own business
___ I consider myself to be strong willed or independent minded

- Kinesthetic learners are "body smart." Movement and hands-on activities help these people learn best. Kinesthetic learners are generally active and animated. Give me examples of people who are kinesthetic learners. *Answers: Athletes, dancers, doctors, and builders.*
- Musical learners are "music smart." Poems, plays, rhythms, rap, chants, and songs are all ways for the music-smart people to learn. Jobs include working as musicians, conductors, orators, and composers.
- Interpersonal learners are "people smart." These learners like people and are generally outgoing and verbal. Discussions of any kind appeal to them. Sales people, politicians, teachers, and social workers are examples of interpersonal learners.
- Intrapersonal learners are "self-smart." These learners tend to love the outdoors and the environment. Most enjoy meditation and journal writing. Psychologists, lawyers, theologians, and counselors tend to be intrapersonal learners.

Closure questions:
- Did your learning style match up with the occupation you have been thinking about?
- What did you learn about yourself? Were you surprised?

Have mentees place their learning style questionnaire in their folder. Have mentees fill in the learning style on their "Future Planning" worksheet, which should be in their folder.

Follow the Leader, Good or Bad?

The thing always happens that you really believe in; and the belief in a thing makes it happen.

—Frank Lloyd Wright

Objective: To identify attributes of a leader and to determine if the leader has a positive or a negative influence.

Materials needed: Whiteboard and markers.

Procedure: Read the quote. Ask mentees what this quote means. The following activity is meant to get your group moving. Please read it carefully as it will require two volunteers.

Ask everyone to stand and arrange themselves in a circle, facing inward. Ask one person to leave the room for a minute. That person will be the guesser for the round. While he or she is gone, the group decides who should be the leader. The leader will be the one who sets the movements for that round. When this person is chosen, invite the guesser to come back. The guesser stands in the very center of the circle.

When the round begins, everyone starts swinging their arms up and down. The leader will eventually begin to do other movements, and everyone else mimics the leader's actions, without being too obvious to reveal who the leader is. The leader can do just about anything he or she wants, such as

- clapping.
- making a kicking motion with his or her leg.
- jumping up and down.
- singing a line from a song.

- patting his or her own head.
- a dance move.

Everyone in the circle should be careful to avoid prolonged eye contact with the leader, so the leader's identity is not given away. The guesser must keep turning his or her head to try to figure out which person is the leader (the person who is starting all of the group's movements). The guesser is allowed to make up to three guesses. If the guess is incorrect, the round continues. If the guess is correct, the leader becomes the new guesser for the next round. If all three guesses are exhausted and the leader is not correctly guessed, the round ends and you can either keep the same guesser or switch it up.

Closure activity:
Write the word *leader* on the board. Have mentees go to the board and write descriptors of that word.

Closure questions:
- Was it easy to identify the leader?
- Does that happen sometimes in life—following but not sure who is leading?
- Give an example of that experience.

What Makes Me Like You?

Tell me and I'll forget; show me and I may remember; involve me and I'll understand.

—Chinese Proverb

Objective: To identify qualities that make a good teacher.

Materials needed: Paper and pencils.

Procedure: Think of a teacher from your past who you think was a *good* teacher. Do not say who it is. Write down the three qualities that made you select that person. (*Some examples are nice, fun, funny, sincere, patient.*) Now, give an example of how that teacher demonstrated that quality. For example, if nice is the quality, saying hello each morning is the action that showed niceness.

Give mentees a few minutes to think and write. While they are working, write the words *teacher* and *mentor* on the board. After mentees complete the first task, have them write the qualities and the associated actions around the words at the board. If mentees identify the same attribute, have them circle the word (so if *nice* is used twice, there should be one circle around that word). After mentees are finished, look at the board.

Discussion questions:
- What are the top three qualities admired by this group?
- Does liking the person mean the person is a good teacher?
- Would the qualities of a liked teacher include these?
- What would you add to the list for a good teacher?
- Can you be a good teacher but not liked? How is that possible?

- According to a college survey, the following attributes are necessary for a
  good teacher:
  Loves to learn and teach.
  Good listening skills.
  Motivating.
  Has sense of humor.
  Knowledgeable.
  Prepared.
  Confident.

When you look back at the qualities you identified as necessary to be a good
teacher, are these on your list? Would you change anything?

Closure questions:
- Is being liked a requirement for good teaching?
- Is being an expert in the area required for good teaching?
- Are the identified qualities important for friends too? Which ones?

I've Got the Spirit

To succeed . . . you need to find something to hold on to, something to motivate you, something to inspire you.

—Tony Dorsett

Objective: To encourage school spirit and to share methods of demonstrating school spirit and celebrating various successes.

Materials needed: Mentee folder, sheet of paper.

Procedure: Have the mentees fill in the following statements:

1. Our school is a *great* school because the students . . . .
2. Our school is a *great* school because the teachers . . . .
3. Our school is a *great* school because in the classes . . . .
4. Our school is a *great* school because the extracurricular activities . . . .

Collect the responses. No names should be on them. Without indicating who said what, read the responses to #1. Have students give a thumbs-up if they agree with what was written to each answer to #1, or a thumbs-down if they disagree. Do the same for #2, #3, and #4.

Discussion questions:
- How do you show school spirit? *Do you go to sports, music, etc. activities? Are you a member of a team or club?*
- Does our school celebrate accomplishments? What types of successes do we celebrate? *Team successes, student successes, individual successes, faculty accomplishments, etc.*
- If not, how could we?

- What can we do to improve school spirit?
- Why is school spirit important?

Closure: Have mentees generate a list of activities in which they have participated or in which they were a spectator.

Mentors should share school spirit thoughts and ideas with the entire staff.

Do You See It My Way?

If you stop learning today, you stop learning tomorrow.

—Howard Hendricks

Objective: To identify school likes and dislikes and to accept these differences in a constructive, positive way.

Materials needed: A sheet of paper and a pen/pencil.

Procedure: Have mentees answer the following on a note card.

- What is your favorite subject this year? Why is it your favorite? (*"The teacher" is not an acceptable response.*)
- What are two of the most important things you learned in that subject?
- What is your least favorite subject this year? Why is it your least favorite? (*"The teacher" is not an acceptable response.*)
- Name two activities you have done in any classes that you have enjoyed.
- What quality do you possess that your teacher might not know? Why don't they know this?

Have the students break into triads and share the responses. Mentors, you can answer the same questions relative to your students—which is your favorite class and why?

Closure questions:
- Would your answers have changed if you could have responded that the teacher is the reason?
- Does the teacher affect your performance? Why or why not?
- Are you good at your favorite subject? Is that why you chose it?

Beating the Bully

Bullies are always cowards at heart and may be credited with a pretty safe instinct in scenting their prey.

—Anna Julia Cooper

Objective: To recognize bullying behaviors and the serious impact they have on the victim.

Materials needed: Paper and pencils.

Procedure: Tell mentees that the data that will be shared are from the National Youth Violence Center. Ask for a volunteer and have her read the following definition.

A person is being bullied when he or she is *exposed, repeatedly and over time, to negative actions on the part of one or more other persons.* Negative action is when a person *intentionally inflicts injury or discomfort upon another person, through physical contact, through words, or in other ways.* Note that bullying can be overt (obvious) or covert (subtle).

The following are examples of bullying behaviors. Remember, bullying is a pattern of behavior that is repeated over time against the same person(s) with a noted power differential.

- Saying hurtful and unpleasant things.
- Making fun of others.
- Using mean and hurtful nicknames.
- Completely overlooking someone.
- Deliberately excluding someone from a group of friends.
- Hitting, kicking, pulling hair, pushing, or shutting a person out,
- Telling lies about a person.

- Spreading false rumors about a person.
- Sending mean notes.
- Trying to get other students to dislike another person.

Ask mentees to
- define what being bullied means.
- give examples of bullying actions.
- assign a percentage (from 0% to 100%) of students who have been bullied or were the bullies. *Answer: Thirty percent of 9–12 graders report or admit being bullied or being the bully.*
- True or False:
  - Males and females bully the same way. *Answer: False.*
  - Both males and females bully by making fun of someone's looks, speech, or behaviors.
  - Males are more likely to get physical by pushing or hitting.
  - Females are more likely to spread rumors or avoid people.

Discussion questions:
- Does any of this information surprise you?
- Did you suspect that males and females bully differently? The same?
- Can you see how social networks such as Facebook could be used in a hurtful way?
- What do you think you can do as individuals?
- What can our high school do as a community to fight bullying?

Closure activity:
Have each mentee write down one way they can help practice non-bullying behaviors.

Friend Request?

Without friends no one would choose to live, though he had all other goods.

—Aristotle

Objective: To set limits regarding Facebook and other social network sites and increase mentee awareness of the potential dangers of these networks. This will improve decision making.

Materials needed: None.

Procedure: This will be a chance for mentees to share with mentors and vice versa. If you do not have a Facebook account, ask your mentees about it. If you do have one, you do not have to disclose this fact. Use your discretion.

Discussion questions:
- How many of you have a Facebook account?
- What is Facebook? *Answer: A social network.*
- How does it work? (*Have mentees answer the question, and add insight if you know something about it.*)
- What are some common words used in Facebook? See if they add more to this basic list.
  Friend—Someone whose friendship you accept or request via the site. The term *friend* can include anyone—boss, pal, stranger, etc.
  Friend request—Notification that someone has asked for your friendship. You can confirm or ignore the request. You can also remove a friend at a later time.
  Gift—Tiny digital e-token you can send a friend. Generally it costs $1.
  Group—Collection of users based on shared interests, activities, etc.

Poke—A slightly annoying way to initiate conversation with another user. Pokes are generally not used by people under 14.

Wall—Space on every user's profile page that allows friends to post messages for the user and every friend of the user to see.

Status Update—What you can type (160 characters maximum) at the top of your profile to let people know what you are thinking, doing, feeling, etc.

Profile—Some information about who you are.

- How does Facebook make money? *Answer: The ads are tailored to the information posted on the profile or on the Facebook account. There are several lawsuits regarding this.*
- Is there a guarantee of privacy on the Internet? *Answer: No.*
- If you delete something on Facebook, is it gone forever? *Answer: No, with tools and skills, a picture you posted can be found by someone. In fact, anything you have posted can be found.*
- Are Facebook accounts being used to check up on you? *Answer: Yes. Recent information suggests that employers are looking at Facebook accounts to see what a prospective employee is like outside the work environment. Some college admissions people have also looked to see what prospective students might be involved in other than what their transcripts or letters of recommendation indicate. If a friend posts a comment about a health issue, that issue can follow a Facebook user for a long time.*
- What are some safety features you can use to protect yourself? *Have mentees generate a list of do's and don'ts for using Facebook—for instance, be careful what you put on your profile page; use firewalls (an anti-virus protection); be aware that you are being marketed; etc.*
- Should you post just any picture? *Discuss the concept of being "tagged."*
- Can someone else take a picture off your Facebook page/profile? *Answer: Yes, anyone can download it to his or her own computer and then use it without you knowing.*
- How many of you can access your Facebook account from your phone?
- How often do you check your Facebook account from school? *Have mentees guess the number of times.*

If you do not know much about Facebook, please let mentees be your guide. They are aware of everything. They also probably will know if you have an account or not.

Closure questions:
- What precautions can you take when using a social network?
- Why is it important to be cautious about what you post on Facebook?

Think Before You Speak

Never be bullied into silence. Never allow yourself to be made a victim.
Accept no one's definition of your life; define yourself.

—Harvey Fierstein

Objective: To recognize that words can be offensive even when that is not the intent and to understand how these words affect the school community; and to see that we are all members of the same community.

Materials needed: Paper, pencil, and access to the Internet if possible.

Procedure: Begin with the following questions:

- What makes a good community? *Answers: Safety, family, friends, people who like you for you, a place to feel welcome, etc.*
- How would you feel if someone were trying to take this community away just because of who you are? *Answers: Angry, hurt, confused, resentful of the people trying to make me feel bad, etc.*
- How does name calling or using derogatory language affect a community? *Answers: It makes people feel bad, makes people seem immature, creates a negative atmosphere; people do not feel safe, comfortable, or welcome; etc.*

Have a mentee read the definition of name calling written below.

Name calling is using a word to link a person to a negative stereotype, idea, or symbol.

Discussion questions:

- Why do people use of derogatory language? *Answers: To intimidate others, to bring them down, to make themselves look more powerful, etc.*

- How does this contribute to a negative community, even if the person calling names believes they are just using these terms to joke around or tease? *You may refer to previous lessons on teasing, bullying, etc.*
- When you hear "that's so gay," "that's so stupid," or "that's retarded," how do you feel?
- What does this have to do with you personally?
- Why is there so much fear and malice surrounding certain words?
- Why does this issue matter to everyone?

Watch the videos found at www.adcouncil.org/default.aspx?id=539. (*Be sure that the link still exists. There are links to three short public-service announcements under "Television" on the right bar of the screen.*)

After watching the videos, have the mentees write

- their first reaction to the public-service announcement (PSA).
- the message of the PSA.

Have a mentee read the following:

On April 6, 2009, an 11-year-old Massachusetts boy, Carl Joseph Walker-Hoover, hanged himself after enduring constant bullying at school, including daily taunts of "gay" and "faggot," despite the fact that he did not identify as gay and his mother's weekly pleas to the school to address the problem.

It was at least the fourth suicide of a middle-school-aged child linked to bullying during the 2008–2009 school year.

AND

This spring, Constance McMillen fought an Itawamba County school board to be able to take her lesbian partner and wear a tuxedo to the Itawamba County Agricultural High School prom, in the small town of Itawamba, Miss., about 20 miles east of Tupelo. The school board responded Wednesday by announcing they were canceling the entire prom, scheduled for April 2. A Feb. 5 memo to students laid out the criteria for bringing a date to the prom, and one requirement was that the person must be of the opposite sex. With all of the media attention, there was an alternative prom planned. All dressed up and ready to join her peers for the event every senior looks forward to since freshman year, Constance was left to feel the joke was on her as she arrived to a prom of seven other students, teacher chaperones, and her principal. Apparently, while Constance and her friends were at what is hard not to coin the "decoy prom," the rest of the school was at another prom reportedly arranged by parents in the community.

(For source and more information, go to www.thinkb4youspeak.com/—again. Check the URL to see if the information is still available.)

Closure Activity:

Read each of these statistics. Ask mentees for their thoughts on this.

86.2% of LGBT students reported being verbally harassed at school.

60.8% of LGBT students felt unsafe at school.

44.1% of LGBT students reported being physically harassed at school.

22.1% of LGBT students reported being physically assaulted at school in the past year.

(Think B4You Speak.)

Ask: What impact do derogatory remarks have on our community?

—Contributed by Kerrigan Mahoney

We Are Family

Remember everyone you meet is fighting a battle—everybody's lonesome.

—Marion Parker

Objective: To recognize we are all members of the same school family and that we have an obligation to help others and seek help when we need it.

Materials needed: None.

Procedure: This activity is called Ups and Downs. Read, "Stand up if you . . ." before each of the bulleted statements. Give a moment after each. You may ask if any mentee has a comment after each statement.

Stand up if you

* know someone who drinks.
* have ever judged a person based on his or her appearance.
* have gone along with something just because it was popular.
* have done volunteer work.
* known someone whose drinking has hurt himself or herself or others.
* have ever lost someone.
* have gotten excited off of some sport or activity.
* have been around someone who has hurt himself or herself.
* have ever felt lonely.

This activity is called Side to Side.

Have mentees move to the left or to the right as indicated. You may ask if any mentee has a comment after each statement.

* Do you think teens are stereotyped? *If yes, move to the right; if no, move to the left.*

- Do you consider yourself with the "majority" or "minority" of teens? *If majority, move to the right; if minority, move to the left.*
- Whose opinion do you value more, friends' or parents'? *If friends, move to the right; if parents, move to the left.*
- Do you ever feel as though you are pressured into compromising who you are in order to be accepted? *If yes, move to the right; if no, move to the left.*
- Which needs improvement, how you treat yourself or how you treat others? *If yourself, move to the right; if others, move to the left.*
- You find out one of your friends is in trouble of some kind. Do you seek help by telling an adult or try to work on it yourself? *If adult, move to the right; if yourself, move to the left.*

Closing comments:
Please know that adults in the building are here to help and assist you. There are times when it is absolutely necessary and appropriate to seek adult help. If someone is threatening to hurt himself or herself or others, or if someone has been inappropriately touched, speak with an adult.

Let's See If What I *Thought* I Was Doing Matches Up with What I *Did*

Success is simple. Do what's right, the right way, at the right time.

—Arnold H. Glasgow

Objective: To reflect and assess so that improvement can take place.

Materials needed: Report cards or progress reports (from guidance), schedules (in mentee folders), and copies of the "Self-Assessment" forms, one for each mentee.

Procedure: Redistribute the mentee folders. Distribute the "Self-Assessment" forms. You will be meeting with each mentee individually. Have the mentee bring the form with him or her. If a self-improvement plan is being designed, have the mentee write the plan down. These meetings should be brief to allow mentees to reflect on, assess, and strategize for improvement. If a mentee is already successful, have a discussion on extracurricular activities. Please follow the following guidelines:

- Have students bring their self-evaluation up with them.
- Be *sensitive* to the situation.
- Keep the discussion *private*. Have mentees in one section of the room and the individual meetings in another.
- The conversation should be 1–2 minutes long per mentee.

Discussion questions:
- What surprised you the most? Why?
- What was your most challenging class? Why?
- What was your favorite class? Why?

- What is one goal you have for improving next term?
- What activities are you involved in?

Closure:
Staple each mentee's self-reflection and report card together and place them in the mentee folder for future reference.

Self-Assessment Worksheet

HOW AM I DOING?

Name _____   Date _____

Projected Graduation Year _____

Objective: To assess your progress after each major evaluation.

For your planning, answer the following questions:

What courses am I doing well in?	Why? What went *right*?

What courses am I having difficulty with?	Why? What went wrong? How can I improve?

Here are two things I will do to improve or maintain my work.

1.

2.

Any other comments, suggestions, or concerns?

R-E-S-P-E-C-T

We have flown the air like birds and swum the sea like fishes, but we have yet to learn the simple act of walking the earth like brothers.

—Reverend Martin Luther King Jr.

Objective: To recognize that bullying behaviors, whether ignored or isolated, cannot be tolerated and are disrespectful.

Materials needed: A piece of paper and pencil.

Procedure: Read the quote of the day, *but do not mention who said it.*

Discussion questions:
- What does the quote mean to you?
- Do you know who the author of the quote is?
- What does the value respect mean to you? (*If the group is having trouble about this value, ask them: What does it "feel" like to be respected? How does respect "look"?*)
- Do you have a close friend who is like a brother or sister to you? (*Some mentees may be only children; you can discuss what attributes make someone "feel" like a sibling.*)
- Even though you might disagree with that person at times, or he or she might get on your nerves, would you help him or her if he or she were in trouble? Why or why not?
- How would you feel if that person were disrespected?
- How do you feel when someone is being bullied, ignored, or isolated?
- Have you ever felt bullied, ignored, or isolated? If yes, describe how you felt and how you rectified the situation.

Martin Luther King Jr. was the author of this quote. Does that surprise you?

Closure activity: Have students break into pairs and share a moment when they felt disrespected. Ask:

- What would have made that moment better?
- What was your reaction to being disrespected? *Answers: Anger, embarrassment, fear, etc.*
- Were those moments examples of being bullied? How so?

Conclude with this statement. Ask mentees if they agree (thumbs up) or disagree (thumbs down) with it.

Respect Is Empowering!

Getting to Know the Man in the Mirror

Things do not change; we change.

—Henry David Thoreau

Objective: To recognize our personal strengths and to be true to ourselves.

Materials needed: A piece of paper and pencil/pen for each mentee and a copy of the poem "The Man in the Mirror," found at www.desitwist.com/english-poetry/man-mirror-17188.html.

Procedure: Explain to mentees that it is time to reflect about ourselves.

- Write down something you are very good at that has nothing to do with school. Then write down the personal skills and qualities that help you do this well. (*For example, dancing; skills: discipline, dedication, agility, the love of it, etc.*)
- Write down something you are not so good at. Write down why you think this is true. (*For example, dancing; not agile, not coordinated, too self-aware, etc.*)

Have mentees break into groups of three and share what they wrote. Go back to the larger group to discuss.

Discussion questions:
- What are some of the qualities that made you good at something?
- What are some of the qualities that made you feel as though you were *not* good at something?
- Do those same qualities show up in your work at school?
- What would you change about your school work if you could?
- What would you keep the same?

Closure activity:
Have a student read the poem "The Man in the Mirror." Ask: How does this poem relate to identifying our own strengths and weaknesses?

Houston, We Have a Problem . . .

> Strength of mind rests in sobriety; for this keeps your reason unclouded by passion.
>
> —Pythagoras

Objective: To identify addictive behaviors, the associated symptoms, and the consequences of those addictions.

Materials needed: None.

Procedure: Have a mentee read the following:

Hello, old friend; I've come to visit once again. I live to see you suffer mentally, physically, spiritually, and socially. I want to make you restless so you can never relax! I want you to be jumpy and nervous and anxious! I want to make you agitated and irritable so everything and everybody make you uncomfortable. I want you to be confused and depressed so that you can't think clearly or positively. I want to make you hate everything and everybody, especially yourself. I want you to feel guilty and remorseful for the things you've done in the past that you'll never be able to let go of. I want to make you angry and hateful toward the world for the way it is and the way you are. I want you to feel sorry for yourself and blame everything but your addiction for the way things are. I want you to be deceitful and untrustworthy, and to manipulate and con as many people as possible. I want to make you fearful and paranoid for no reason at all. I want you to wake up during all hours of the night and scream for me. You know you can't sleep without me. I'm even in your dreams.

I want to be the first thing you wake up to every morning and the last thing you touch before you pass out. I would rather kill you, but I'll be happy enough just to put you back in the hospital, another institution or jail. But you know I'll still be waiting for you when you get out. I love to watch you slowly going insane. I love to see all the physical damage I am causing you. I can't help but sneer and chuckle when you shiver and shake, when you freeze and sweat at the same time, and when you wake with your sheets and blankets soaking wet. It's amusing to watch you make love to the toilet bowl—heaving and retching and not able to hold me down. It's amazing how much destruction I can do to your internal organs while at the same time work on your brain, destroying it bit by bit. I deeply appreciate how much you sacrifice for me. The countless good jobs you've sacrificed for me. All the fine friends that you deeply cared for—you gave up for me. And what's more, the ones you turned against yourself because of your inexcusable actions. I'm even more grateful.

And especially, your loved ones, your family, the most important people in the world to you—you even threw away for me. I cannot express in words the gratitude I have for the loyalty and respect you have for me—you sacrificed all these beautiful things in life just to devote yourself completely to me. But do not despair, my friend, for on me you may always depend. For after you have lost all of these things, you can still depend on me to take even more! You can depend on me to keep you in living hell, to keep in your mind, body and soul; for I will not be satisfied until you are dead, my friend.

—*Anonymous*

Pause here before continuing.

Ask: Who is the narrator of this writing? *Answers: My name is: crack, alcohol, weed, coke, "h," dust, uppers, oxy, and so on.*

Give mentees a few minutes to think about this reading.

Discussion questions:
- What is the first thing you think of when you hear the word *addiction*? *Answers: Drugs, alcohol, etc.*
- What would you add if you knew addiction is defined as compulsive patterns of behavior? *Answers: Gambling, eating disorders, shopping, etc.*

There are certain prevalent behaviors among addicts that strongly indicate a problem.

Symptom #1
    Unable to meet responsibilities at home, school, or office.

Symptom #2
    Continues to use substances or engage in behavior even when it is dangerous.

Symptom #3

The need increases to engage in behavior or use more of a substance to achieve the same effect or feeling.

Symptom #4

Has tried but failed to stop using the substance or end the behavior.

Symptom #5

Continues to engage in the behavior or use the substances after they have been caught or confronted.

Answering yes to three or more of the above symptoms during a 12-month period may show that you or a loved one has an addiction. The first step to treating an addiction is recognizing that it exists.

Closure:

Remind mentees that if they know of anyone who demonstrates any of these destructive behaviors, they should seek out an adult who can help. Ask mentees to identify a behavior that might be an indicator of addiction.

Embrace Change

You must take personal responsibility. You cannot change the circumstances, the seasons, or the wind, but you can change yourself. That is something you have charge of.

—Jim Rohn

Objective: To recognize that change helps define who we are and that our reaction and attitude determines how we will handle change in the future.

Materials needed: Paper and pencil.

Procedure: Have mentees write down their answers to the following questions.

- Name four significant changes that have occurred in your life. (*Examples: going from elementary school to middle school, from middle school to high school, etc.*)
- How did you feel about those changes?
- Did you have a say in these changes? If yes, how so? If no, why not?
- What feelings are generally associated with any change?
- When you find a seat for the first time in any class, do you return to that same seat the next time the class meets? Why or why not?
- If someone is sitting in your seat—whether in a class, in the cafeteria or on the bus—how do you react?

After mentees have finished answering, have them pair with someone they have not yet paired with. Answer each question. Rejoin the group. Have each member of the pair share an experience.

Closure questions:
• Are there similarities in all areas involving a major change?
• Are there any similarities in the feelings associated with change?
• What changes frighten you?
• What change may excite you?
• How do you cope with those major changes?
• What are some ways we can make change easier?

On Your Mark, Get Set, and GO!

My great concern is not whether you have failed, but whether you are content with your failure.

—Abraham Lincoln

Objective: To look at various studying techniques.

Materials needed: None.

Procedure: Have mentees do the following quickly. This activity should not take long.

- Clasp your hands together and fold the thumbs across the top, is your right or left thumb on top? Who has the right one on top? Left?
- Fold your arms across your chest. Is your right or left arm on top? Who has the right one? Left?
- Which leg do you put into your pants first? Who puts the right one in first? Left?
- Which eye do you prefer to wink with? Who winks with the right one? With the left one?
- Which side of the bed do you get out of in the morning? Who gets out of the right side? Left side?
- Can you roll your tongue? Who can? Can't?

Discussion questions:
- What is the purpose of this activity?
- Did everyone have the same strengths or weaknesses?
- Do we approach a task in the same manner?
- How do you prepare for tests, exams, or standardized assessments?

- Do you study the night before or do you start studying long before the exams?
- Do you study differently for different subjects? Ask for examples.

Give these suggestions to all mentees:

Assessment preparation:

- Review notes/work.
- Form study groups.
- Studying in the day (before dark) is statistically better than studying at night.
- Study in chunks.
- Eat a good breakfast before exams.
- Get a good night's sleep.
- If you have prepared, you will be less likely to be anxious.
- Look over the exam **before** you begin.
- Pace yourself on the exam. If you do not know something, move on and go back to that point later.
- Think of a comfortable place.
- Be prepared by practicing!
- Be confident.

Closure questions:
- Which activities match up with your learning style?
- Which don't?
- What works best for you?

I'm Just *Teasing!* I'm Only *Kidding!* *Relax,* He Knows I'm Kidding!

Never be bullied into silence. Never allow yourself to be made a victim. Accept no one's definition of your life; define yourself.

—Harvey Fierstein

Objective: To recognize that teasing can cross the line, can hurt others' feelings, and can become bullying.

Materials needed: Chalk (markers) and board. If you have enough markers, distribute one to each, otherwise just pass the marker around.

Procedure: Explain to mentees that this session involves an activity called Chalk Talk. This is a silent activity that will allow them to generate ideas about a certain topic. You will write a word on the board and give each mentee an opportunity to write a word or words they feel relate to this topic. You will occasionally write a question next to the word or comment. You may also draw lines to show relationships between the words. *Remember,* this is a silent activity.

Write the word *teasing* on the board. Allow mentees to go up and write around that word. If a particular word or phrase needs clarification, you may write a statement or ask a question. This allows for the writer to respond. Remind mentees that this is a silent process. This activity can take a while as you must give the mentees time to process. Be patient.

Come back to a circle.

Discussion questions:
- What would be a good definition of teasing?
- How does it feel when you get teased?

- Does it feel different under different circumstances?
- When does teasing become bullying?

Closure questions:
- Look at the Chalk Talk board. How does it make you feel when you read it?
- Let's make an effort to see how people respond when we are teasing them.

I'm Ready to Explode!

The refusal to listen is the first step towards violence.

—Martin Luther King Jr.

Objective: To identify stressors and recognize when you are getting angry will allow you to think before you react.

Materials needed: Paper, pencil, marker, and board.

Procedure: Begin the conversation by saying, "Finding words to correctly understand how we feel is challenging. Being 'mad' doesn't always say what we want it to say. Often, it means we are hurt. Sometimes it means we are offended. Other times it means we are frustrated. Reacting to that 'mad' feeling can lead to new problems and, therefore, new feelings. Our bodies do respond when we are getting upset. Let's begin to dialogue about recognizing triggers and physical responses to anger and coping with them."

After distributing the paper and pencil, have mentees fill in the blanks.

- When people start to feel angry, they usually feel it in parts of their body. These are (d)anger signals. When I feel angry, my danger signals are. . . .
- When I'm angry my body lets me know by. . . . .
- When I'm angry, I usually. . . .
- One thing I like about how I handle anger is. . . . .
- Two things I'd do differently when I'm angry are. . . .
- Three things I can say to myself to calm myself are. . . . .
- When have you had conflicting feelings, such as *excitement* and *fear,* at the same time? An example would be if you were performing on stage and you were excited, but frightened. Think of experiences in which you had

multiple and conflicting emotions. Which feeling had more influence on your choices? How did your body feel? What was the result?

Ask for a volunteer to generate a list for each bullet. Have the volunteer write the lists on the board.

Closure comments and activity:
Recognizing the signals your body sends is important in "thinking" before reacting. What could you do to slow down your response to anger? Write the word *cope* on the board. Have mentees write coping skills around that word.

I'm Still Stressing . . .

If you can find a path with no obstacles, it probably doesn't lead anywhere.

—Frank A. Clark

Objective: To recognize stressful feelings and learn implementation strategies to help reduce stress.

Materials needed: Paper and pencil.

Procedure: Remind mentees about the session on anger. Ask them what they remember about that session.

- What were some of the physical responses to anger?
- What did anger "feel" like?

Have mentees take a piece of paper and answer the following questions:

- Have you ever done or said something stupid while angry?
- What was it?
- Have you ever ignored something that *made* you angry?
- How did that feel?
- What things have you done *well* while you were angry?
- Name three ways to cope when stressed or angry.

Have mentees share answers to these questions. When finished, read the following coping and stress-reducing strategies:

1. When you feel stressed, practice taking long, deep breaths.
2. Take regular breaks from your work.
3. Get regular exercise. Try to exercise for a minimum of 20 minutes three times per week.
4. Eat a balanced diet.

5. Avoid caffeine, which is a stimulant.
6. Avoid depending on drugs and alcohol to help you relax. This can quickly become a crutch.
7. Learn time management and organization skills.
8. Use humor to lighten difficult situations.
9. Seek to find the positive in every situation. View adversity as an opportunity for learning and growth.
10. Do not bury your emotions. This is a temporary fix at best. Unresolved emotions can resurface as nightmares or physical illness.
11. If you find that a relationship stresses you out, end it, if possible. If it is not possible, remember that you may not be in control of other people's behavior, but you are in control of how you react to it.
12. Give compliments freely and smile often. You will be amazed how the mood around you will change and how in turn you will feel better.
13. Learn to really listen to what others are saying rather than getting upset because you disagree. Seek to find areas of common ground and work for a compromise.

Closure questions and activity:
• Are there any other strategies to reduce stress you could add to this list?
• Which strategy have you already used?

Ask mentees to commit to trying one *new* stress reduction strategy when they are feeling angry or overwhelmed.

You're in Charge

Never trust anything that can think for itself if you can't see where it keeps its brain.

—J.K. Rowling

Objective: To give mentees some choice in mentoring sessions.

Materials needed: A box of some type, paper, and pencils.

Procedure: Mentors begin the discussion about open forum.

Let's explore the idea of an open forum. This will involve setting up guidelines for all discussions. An open forum will mean mentees can choose topics for discussion. The topic (or topics) will be written down on a piece of paper and placed in an envelope or a box of your choosing. (*Mentors, you must determine your comfort level regarding topics for discussion.*)

Have mentees anonymously write the issue to be discussed on a blank sheet of paper. Then place the paper in a box.

Set up guidelines for the open forum. Some ideas include

- how to choose the topic.
- how to recognize that a mentee wants to speak.
- limit comments.
- during the open forum, mentees use acquired listening skills (*learned in previous sessions*) and try to refrain from comments except in extreme cases.
- civility of language (*no disrespectful comments or comments of a personal nature*).
- no off-topic discussions.
- no sidebar discussions.

Once all are comfortable with the guidelines, try the open-forum process. Pick a topic out of the box, and have a conversation modeling the rules for discussion. Here are a few other topics for consideration: eating disorders, school policy and rules, Internet slander, teenage pregnancy, sexually trans- mitted diseases, current events, etc.

Closure:

An open-forum lesson can be used whenever there is down time in a session.

Hey, Thanks!

As we express our gratitude, we must never forget that the highest appreciation is not to utter words, but to live by them.

—John Fitzgerald Kennedy

Objective: To recognize and thank people who have made a difference in our lives, which reinforces positive behaviors.

Materials needed: Paper and pencil.

Procedure: Ask these questions allowing enough time for mentees to respond.

- If you had one hour to live, who would you call?
- Why would you call that person?
- What would you say?
- Have you considered calling that person and saying what you wanted to say?

Go around the group and ask if anyone wanted to share his or her answers. This is a very personal session; therefore, give the opportunity to share but allow mentees a "pass."

Ask mentees to write the answer to the following:

- List 10 things for which you are grateful.
- Describe one of the most beautiful things that you have ever seen.
- How can you show your gratitude to a teacher, coach, or classmate?
- Commit to saying "thank you" to someone in the building who has made a difference in your life. Consider writing a note to that person.

Go around the group and ask each mentee to share two things for which he or she is grateful.

Closure activity:

Have a mentee read the following quote:

> At times our own light goes out and is rekindled by a spark from another person. Each of us has cause to think with deep gratitude of those who have lighted the flame within us.

—Albert Schweitzer

Ask: Who sparked the flame in your life? Why?

See the Glass Half Full

Look within! . . . The secret is inside you.

—Dajian Huineng

Objective: To allow each mentee to see the good in others and share positive attributes about one another. To recognize that all people have positive attributes to share with the world.

Materials needed: Multicolored construction paper for each mentee and for the mentor, and magic markers or colored pencils.

Procedure: Distribute a piece of construction paper and marker to each mentee.

Have each mentee print his or her name in the center of the paper. Explain that these sheets will be passed around to each member of the group. Each mentee should write a word or phrase that expresses something he or she has learned about that person or a quality that he or she likes about that person. These comments should be positive in nature. Mentees should *think* about what they will write, and be honest.

After everyone is finished, return the sheet to that individual. Allow time for mentees to read and process what others have written.

Closure activity:

Have mentees come up with two activities that would help the group bond better. Mentors should share these results with colleagues.

If You Can Dream It, You Can Achieve It

Your belief determines your action and your action determines your results, but first you have to believe.

—Mark Victor Hansen

Objective: By identifying and verbalizing our strengths and weaknesses, we can learn more about ourselves and about others.

Materials needed: Copies of "If You Can Dream It" questionnaire, paper, and pencils. *Different questions will be distributed to each mentee within the pair so that each will be asked different questions.*

Procedure: Group mentees in pairs using one of the pairing methods described in the opening chapter. Explain to mentees that this activity will be conducted as though they were in a job interview. Each mentee in the pair will ask the other mentee a set of questions. Then roles will be reversed and the questioner will be the one who answers. Allow time for a little discussion. Encourage questioners to ask follow-up questions if appropriate. For example, if a mentee's strength is that he or she is very organized, a follow-up question could be, "Can you give me an example?" Distribute a set of questions to each mentee and begin.

Bring the group back together. Go around the circle and ask each mentee for one of their strengths.

Discussion questions:
- Which was harder, identifying your strengths or your weaknesses? Why?
- What did you learn from this activity?
- What did you learn about the other person in your pair?
- Were you comfortable talking about your weaknesses? Why or why not?

Closure activity:

Distribute paper and pencil. Have mentees list their strengths. They may include things they had not thought of in the initial activity. Now make a list of at least five things you like doing. Go around the group and ask mentees if their list of strengths relate to the list of things they like to do.

"If You Can Dream It . . ."
Questionnaire

Questionnaire #1

1. Name three of your strengths.

2. Name three of your weaknesses.

3. Describe your typical day.

4. What was a major problem you had and how did you go about handling it?

Questionnaire #2

1. Tell me a little about yourself.

2. Give me an example of something that motivates you and explain why that motivates you.

3. If I asked your best friend or your teacher to describe your strengths, what would he or she say?

4. What character trait do you need to improve and why?

Am I Heading in the Right Direction?

You must be the change you want to see in the world.

—Mahatma Gandhi

Objective: To reflect on the past and to commit to making one change for the future.

Materials needed: Mentee folders and a copy the Final Reflection worksheet for each mentee.

Procedure: Distribute the mentee folders. Distribute the Final Reflection worksheets and have mentees complete them. Give them time to reflect over the program. Explain that now is a time for self-reflection about performance over time. After they have finished, ask all to come back to the circle.

Discussion questions:
- What is one thing you will change about yourself for next year?
- Name one challenge you hope to overcome next year.
- What one quality will you work on improving next year?

Closure questions:
- What does mentoring mean to you?
- What were the goals of the mentoring program?
- Were those goals accomplished?
- What have you learned about mentoring?
- Were you able to improve your grades over time?
- What one thing have you learned over this past year?

Have mentees return all their worksheets to their folders. Collect them and hold on to them for next year.

119

Final Reflection Worksheet

Name _____   Year _____

Please answer the following questions:

1. What have you learned about yourself over the past year?

2. Name something you were proud of in the past year.

3. What is something you could have done better this year?

4. What steps did you take to improve yourself?

5. Your final grades will appear on your transcript. What do you think people will think about you up to this point?

6. What one thing will you try to do better for next year? How will that help you?

Who Am I?

Success is to be measured not so much by the position that one has reached in life as by the obstacles which he has overcome while trying to succeed.

—Booker T. Washington

It is a terrible thing to see and have no vision.

—Helen Keller

Objective: To recognize that bias and discrimination exist in many ways but together we can make a change.

Materials needed: Internet access if desired.

Procedure: If you have Internet access, you can have pictures of the following people already on the screen. If not, simply read the names and their contributions.

Frederick Jones: air conditioner
Alice Parker: heating furnace
Walter Sammons: comb
Lydia O. Newman: brush
Sarah Boone: ironing board
George T. Samon: clothes dryer
Dr. Charles Drew: scientist who found a way to preserve and store blood. He worked with blood transfusions and started the world's first blood bank. He died from being denied access to his own invention in a racist hospital.

Augustus Jackson: ice cream

Alexander Miles: elevator

All of these people are men and women of color. Black History Month has been taking place since 1926. It was originally named Negro History week. The purpose is to celebrate all types of people and their contributions. Barbara Jordan, a Texas politician and a black woman, said, "Do not call for black power or green power. Call for *brain* power."

Discussion questions:

- What do you think Barbara Jordan meant by this?
- Is racism present here? If yes, cite an example.
- Are there other prejudices besides racism? *Answers: Ethnic, religious, gender, etc.*
- Who was Helen Keller? *Answer: A young woman who was deaf, dumb, and blind.* Did she experience any bias?
- Do people of color as well as people with any disability have similar challenges?
- How are those challenges the same?
- How are they different?
- How can we work to improve the situation?
- Does attitude make a difference?
- What does enabling mean?

Closure activity:

Write the word *prejudice* on the board. Have mentees take turns and write ways to combat prejudice in our community.

I Can Get You to Say Anything . . .

Anything worth having is worth working for.

—Andrew Carnegie

Objective: To improve questioning techniques and increase awareness of how to search for information, which will give opportunity to find solutions to other problems.

Materials needed: Sticky notes and pencils.

Procedure: Have mentees think of a famous person. This person must be someone everyone in the group will know. Distribute one sticky note to each person. Each mentee secretly writes the name of a famous person on that sticky note. While keeping the name hidden, mentees should stick the note to another mentee's forehead. Each mentee will get a chance to ask the group questions to help him or her figure out who the unknown person on his or her forehead is. Only questions to which the answer is yes or no may be asked. For example:

- Am I alive?
- Am I female?

If the response to the mentee's question is no, his or her turn is over. If the answer to the questions is yes, the mentee can continue asking questions to determine who is on his or her forehead. Mentees keep asking questions until a no answer is received or the mentee makes a guess at who the famous person is. If a mentee guesses correctly, he or she wins the round but the game continues until all mentees know their secret identity. If the mentee's guess is wrong, his or her turn is over.

Closure questions:
- Was it difficult to figure out questions to ask that gave only a yes or no answer?
- How could you narrow down the number of questions?
- Would it be more challenging if you were only allowed a few questions?
- Did anyone in the group pose interesting questions?
- How do you know if a question was a good one or not?
- When trying to solve a problem, do you use similar strategies?
- If a teacher presents a lesson and you are confused, what would you do to get clarification?